TABLE OF CONTENTS

Preface ix

LESSON 1: Two Perspectives—Michael's Story 1
    The Boss's Perspective 3
    The Shocking, Surprising Statistics............. 4
    A Different Way of Looking at Management...... 5

LESSON 2: Why Do Blue Collar Managers Matter?... 9
    Who Are Blue-Collar People?.................... 9
    Why Blue-Collar Management Matters 12
    Some Say Blue-Collar People Can't Cut It as
    Managers....................................... 14
    Manager or Messenger?........................ 20
    A Word About Blue-Collar Women 21
    Why Working Supervisors Have Multiple
    Personalities................................... 22
    The Peter Principle Is Still Right—But 24
    Management Is Still a Craft..................... 24
    When Should You Train?........................ 25
    Which Sounds Best? To Be Mediocre or To Be a
    Force Multiplier?............................... 28

LESSON 3: They Don't Talk About Management By
Gunpoint... 31

LESSON 4: The Underpinning of Management and
Leadership—Communication......................... 37
    The Definition of Communication Is Incomplete .. 38

What Causes Misunderstanding? 39
No, They Really Weren't Born to Piss You Off 41
Behavior—How People Do Things............... 42
How Behavior Affects Communication.......... 44
Misunderstanding Can Kill 48
The Big Myth about the Words We Use.......... 49
What You Can Do................................ 51

LESSON 5: The Keys to Success are Rarely in a Job Description 55
Agreements Create Accountability.............. 58
Accountability Requires Agreement............. 60
Scrapping the Annual Review Makes Accountability Easier........................... 62

LESSON 6: The Road to Success is Paved with Indecisive Squirrels 65
Drilling Down on Decision-Making 65
What Are Good Decisions? 69
Dealing with the Emotions of Decision-Making .. 69
Screw the Facts! Let's Just Argue 70
The Process and Experience Are as Important as the Information 71
No Consequences Lead to Poor Decisions 73
Failure Will Happen—Here's How to Deal with It. .. 74

LESSON 7: Think Strategically—Act Tactically....... 77
Firefighting at Work and in The Wild............ 79
Firefighting is Sexy, But It Doesn't Get the Job Done.. 80
What Are They Avoiding?....................... 82

THEY'RE MANAGERS ▶ NOW WHAT?

How to Develop **Blue Collar Managers** and **Supervisors**

BART GRAGG

INDIE BOOKS INTERNATIONAL

Copyright © 2018 by Bart Gragg
All rights reserved.
Printed in the United States of America.

No part of this publication may be reproduced or distributed in any form or by any means without the prior permission of the publisher. Requests for permission should be directed to permissions@indiebooksintl.com, or mailed to Permissions, Indie Books International, 2424 Vista Way, Suite 316, Oceanside, CA 92054

Neither the publisher nor the author is engaged in rendering legal or other professional services through this book. If expert assistance is required, the services of appropriate professionals should be sought. The publisher and the author shall have neither liability nor responsibility to any person or entity with respect to any loss or damage caused directly or indirectly by the information in this publication.

Additional Copyrights and Trademark References: Blue Collar University® is a Registered Trademark of the author, Bart Gragg. (While it is not an accredited institute of higher education, it is a method and a place for increasing the education and skill level of management and supervision, regardless the level.) The One Page Business Plan® is a Registered Trademark of The One Page Business Plan Co., Berkeley, CA.

ISBN-10: 1-947480-37-5
ISBN-13: 978-1-947480-37-7
Library of Congress Control Number: 2018963538

Designed by Joni McPherson, mcphersongraphics.com

INDIE BOOKS INTERNATIONAL, LLC
2424 VISTA WAY, SUITE 316
OCEANSIDE, CA 92054

www.indiebooksintl.com

Dedicated to all managers and business owners looking for a place to start developing their management and supervision.

I understand your frustration and your care, and I hope this book helps.

With special thanks...

It's been said that anyone that ever accomplished anything of significance had a companion just outside of the limelight. For me, that person is Beth Mermann. This book would have taken a decade longer to complete had it not been for her encouragement. Beth's companionship, wisdom, intellect, probing questions, and meaningful conversations have been a great source of inspiration for me.

Thank you, Beth, from the bottom of my heart.

Fire Prevention is Not Sexy—But It Pays the Bills... 84

LESSON 8: Piss-Poor Planning on Your Part Does Not Make It an Emergency on My Part 85
    How to Plan Properly........................... 85
    If They Can't Gantt, Teach Them................ 88
    The Perils of Planning......................... 89
    Why People Dislike Planning 90

LESSON 9: Does Safety Really Begin With Leadership?... 93
    Culture—Not Just Important to Yogurt 94
    Change from "Who" to "How?".................. 95

LESSON 10: Observations From the Field 99
    They're Managers—Now What?................. 99
    Management Styles 99
    On Training Blue Collar Managers and Supervisors................................... 100
    How People Learn............................ 101

LESSON 11: Selecting for Success.................. 107
    The Core of the Selection Process 110
    What If They Can't Hack It? 112

Resources 115

About the Author 119

› PREFACE ‹

I hesitate to use the terms "white collar" and "blue collar" together, as it feels like I am talking about a class system, which, in fact, our society has created. But that has been divisive, and my goal is to reduce the "us-versus-them" factions created by that system. Please trust that when I use those terms, I am merely using them as descriptors for the two types of work we are discussing.

In writing, it is difficult to balance "he" and "she" and "us" and "them." I use "he" and "she" interchangeably, with no disrespect intended to either gender.

We don't need a government study to tell us that there are certain things people really want in life, and especially at work. People want:

- Respect and dignity: to not be shamed, to not be made fun of
- To be asked, not told
- To know the reasons why they are being asked to do something
- Encouragement, even when they fail
- Some control over the decisions that affect their work and future

At work, if not in every other area of life, people also want:
- Clarity about what is required of them
- Accountability for themselves as well as their peers and bosses
- The ability to give input on the products, processes, and production they are involved in

These are all concepts that are easy enough to recognize, but not always easy to carry out.

Management, at its core, is the result of two things: conversations and decisions. In this book I talk about communication being the underpinning of good management; conversations with peers, employees, bosses, vendors, and so forth take communication to a whole new level. Conversations, as opposed to memos and edicts, can be safer, allow for disagreement, and promote agreement. Decisions are the results of those conversations. "What do you see that needs to be done? How do we accomplish that?"

Creating change in people takes effort—more so because if you want someone to change, you are going to have to change first. This is the opposite of the way we view our relationship to subordinates. We think they should change to meet us where we are. But it doesn't work that way. We will need to lead the change by changing first, leading by example, and then teaching managers and supervisors (effectively our students) to follow our example.

Change gets trickier when people move from labor into management ("labor" can mean anything from a heavy equipment operator to a software programmer). Hopefully, this book will help you gain a new perspective of those changes and give you some guidance about how to implement them.

- Change doesn't happen until someone takes action; it would be better if you were that someone.
- Creating change requires effort up front, reflection, and reinforcement to push through.
- If you want your managers and supervisors to change, you will need to change first.
- Lasting change takes time.

›LESSON 1‹

Two Perspectives—Michael's Story

In 2006, the telephone rang, and I could hear the panic in Michael's voice on the other end. He was a young man at the time, and his life to that point hadn't been the greatest. With parents who weren't the best role models, two early marriages that ended in divorce, children from each, and encounters with the law, Michael was now married to the love of his life, with another child to care for, and he had never given up trying to better himself. Michael had worked his way up from laborer to apprentice to journeyman pipe fitter. He was then promoted to manager because he was really good at his job, technically.

Michael said, "I think my boss is going to fire me."

I asked why he thought that.

He said, "I have been the manager of my department for over a year now and just received my first evaluation. Here is what it said: 'Michael has met none of the criteria for being a manager in this company. He has ninety days to get his act together.' That was it. That was all it said."

I asked Michael, "What are the criteria?"

"I don't know the criteria!" he answered. "Can you help me?"

When we met the next day, I asked him, "What do you most want from this job?"

He said, "Respect. Respect for a job well done."

"What does respect look like to you?" I probed.

"I want my boss's boss to come to my office and tell me I am doing a great job."

I then handed Michael a spiral notebook and said, "You know how in the trades you use duct tape to fix things? Management is your new trade—you have to develop it like any other set of skills. And that notebook is the next level of duct tape. Used properly, it will fix many things."

The rules for using the notebook are:

- Document everything as soon as it happens.
- Whenever you have a task to do, a phone call to return, a part to order, or anything that needs to be done at work, you write it down in that notebook.
- Always skip three lines before you write the next task down. Those blanks are for documenting any actions you need to take or that you did take. If it isn't documented, it didn't happen.
- When you complete a task, you draw one line through it or make a mark next to it so you can still read it and reference it in the future.
- That notebook is *always* with you.

The next step was to figure out what the criteria for success were. Like so many of us, Michael didn't want to admit to his boss that he needed help, so this wasn't going to be easy.

The Boss's Perspective

At this point in the story, let's step back and take a look at the situation from the perspective of Michael's boss. We'll call him Tom.

Was it that Tom didn't know the criteria for Michael's success? Was it that he didn't care about Michael's success? Was it that Tom did what so many managers do and took the easy way out during the annual review? If any of those were true, *why* were they true?

My bet: Tom didn't know how to help Michael. It wasn't that Tom was a bad person. It was that Tom wasn't a good boss. Just as Michael's job was to support his people, Tom's job was to support Michael. He wasn't a good boss because he didn't know the criteria for supporting Michael.

With a little coaching, Michael began having conversations with everyone at work who might have an opinion about what his job was. Eventually, he gathered a list of specific items he needed to work on, such as returning phone calls, emails, handling logistics, planning, prioritizing, and getting paperwork and reports done in a timely manner.

Michael has since moved up from department manager to branch manager. He has survived a corporate buyout and manages a territory serving a quarter of the state of California. He is now training managers, and by the way, he shows them how to use a notebook. No, the notebook wasn't the only thing that changed in his performance as a manager, but it was key to the process.

When asked what the best part of this journey was, Michael answers, "Respect. People respect me now, for what I do and how I do it."

In 2006, I created Blue Collar University to help blue-collar managers and supervisors like Michael be successful. It is extremely difficult for them to do well when they are asked to do it alone and under the pressure to which they are subjected.

I wrote this book to help business owners, executives, and managers at all levels better understand how to prepare, support, and develop blue-collar managers and supervisors. It will also show you how to get rid of the dreaded annual review, how to stop the conflict that comes with "us versus them," and how to be able to manage by fact.

The Shocking, Surprising Statistics

Would it surprise you to know that research shows that as many as 60 percent of managers fail within the first twenty-four months of their having assumed the position?

In proprietary research of nearly 100 organizations that have a blue-collar support component, not one of them knew what percentage of their blue-collar managers and supervisors were failing. Some of them did sense that failure was an issue which needed to be addressed. This research raised the following flags:

- How many blue-collar managers and supervisors (initially) fail?
- Why do so many blue-collar managers and supervisors fail?
- Why does it take twenty-four months to know they are failing?
- How many managers are Retired in Place (R.I.P.)?
- How can we help these managers understand what success looks like?

A Different Way of Looking at Management

To understand why managers fail and what helps them achieve success, let me share with you this crazy idea: Why don't we treat management as a partnership?

When we look at management as a partnership, then we can talk about the three critical components of any successful partnership:

1. Agreement
2. Accountability
3. Respect

Michael, and others like him, fail because they lack those three cornerstones of success. They don't know management's criteria for success, and just as important, they don't have the opportunity to agree on those criteria. Having agreement makes it easier to hold people accountable up and down the food chain. When agreement and accountability exist, they foster respect.

What is one of the first signs of the end of a relationship or partnership? When one person shows contempt for the other. What is the opposite of contempt? Respect.

Agreement and accountability foster respect.

Like a three-legged stool, if you cut off any one of these components, the whole thing collapses.

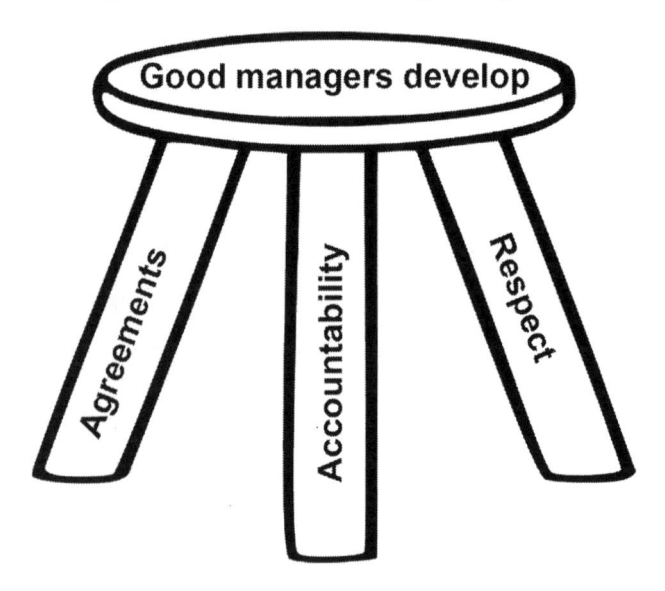

Good managers develop
Agreements | Accountability | Respect

The problems begin with the promotion of labor into management, which is a *really good* strategy when it's executed properly. The top two reasons people are promoted from skilled labor to management are because they are good at their technical level, and someone likes them.

To understand why the transition from labor to management can be such a struggle, we need to talk about who blue-collar managers are and the changes they go through during and after promotion.

- Remember that there are always two perspectives—yours and theirs.
- Unless you take time to think about what success looks like for them, from their perspective, and have a conversation with them about it, their perspectives will not match yours.
- Upper management needs to look at managers and supervisors as partners.
- For best results, create agreements, hold them accountable, and be accountable to them.
- Do all of this with respect.

⟩ LESSON 2 ⟨

Why Do Blue Collar Managers Matter?

Who Are Blue-Collar People?

Most people have an intuitive sense of who blue-collar people are. They can point out the blue-collar people in their lives. They offer job titles such as machinist, plumber, electrician, carpenter, sergeant, police officer, firefighter, laborer, pool cleaner, chimney sweep, crane operator, assembler, mechanic, and so on, as if a career defines who anyone is. When pressed for a definition, they answer with a description of the job duties performed. The answers aren't about *who* blue-collar people are; rather, the answers are about *what they do*.

Pressed further, they talk about people who have no higher education, no ability to learn things other than "hard skills," such as turning a wrench, driving a forklift, or hunting and fishing. People even say that blue-collar workers will do the jobs no one else will.

Nothing could be further from the truth.

Blue-collar people are fathers and mothers, husbands and wives, brothers and sisters, sons and daughters. They have hopes and dreams, and they fight the daily battles that all of us fight; to feed, clothe, and house their families, and to educate their children. They do some jobs that others will not, and some that others *cannot*. They feed us and fuel our cars; they move products and produce; they explore for and deliver energy; they keep planes in the air and cars on the road.

Most of all, though, blue-collar people are human beings, which means they have something in common with all of us—they use their brains.

Blue-collar people are teachable and interested in learning. I know many blue-collar people who have Bachelor's degrees, more than a few with a Master's degree, and several with PhDs. Indeed, most blue-collar companies were created by a blue-collar person. Look around you at construction companies, electricians, plumbers, agricultural businesses. Chances are extremely likely that the founder was blue-collar, working in that industry and either had a better idea about that business service or product or felt she could run a business more effectively and keep more of the dollars.

Many choose to continue to work in blue-collar roles because, in the words of a Marine Corps gunnery sergeant who, when asked why he didn't become an officer, replied, "I don't want to put up with the bullsh*t."

But what do we really mean when we say "blue-collar people"?

Instead of defining them by the roles they occupy or the tasks that they perform, look at this perspective: we are talking about people who *work primarily with tools and objects*, even though they do this in concert with people and data.

When they are promoted to supervision or management, they shift their responsibilities to working *primarily with people and data*.

Blue-collar managers and supervisors move from working primarily with tools and objects to working primarily with people and data.

This shift requires them to use parts of the brain that are different from those used for their former tasks.

When we promote blue-collar people to leadership roles, we are asking them to rewire their brains. As people move from labor into management, who and what they work with changes. Therefore, how they work and how they learn changes dramatically.

Becky, a bakery manager, was telling me about her friends who want to go to her house during the holidays. Their reasoning was because she manages a bakery she must be an incredible baker. While Becky is good at baking some things (she did come up through the ranks), this does not include holiday cakes and cookies. Just because she runs the department, that doesn't mean her home always smells like Christmas.

Here is Becky's (verbatim) reply to her friends:

> *I DON'T BAKE!!! Why is it that everyone is soooo amused that I cannot bake? Just because I wear a badge that says Bakery Manager on it doesn't make me some kind of "master baker"!?!? At home everything that goes in my oven burns. (Kidding!) I haven't burnt the ice cream because it doesn't go in the oven. At work? I lead people. I manage numbers and product. And I solve problems! I. DO. NOT. BAKE! — Becky C.*

Why Blue-Collar Management Matters

Why does blue-collar management matter? It is simple, really. While the business of being a manager can be complex, the bottom line is that management is about making decisions such as what to sell, where to ship it, when to deliver it, why *that* particular item should be in *that* particular market, along with how to produce, package, store, maintain, and manage inventory.

The level of management at which a decision is made doesn't matter. The complexity of the decision doesn't matter. What matters is the resulting impact of the decision.

Every manager at every level has the potential to make decisions that affect morale, production, safety, and innovation, all of which affect the bottom line.

Here's a real-life example. (The industry has been changed to protect the innocent.) A business owner decides he wants to expand the company service line. The company's mainstay is logging timber. A salesperson convinces the owner there is a market for rare hardwoods that can be recovered from river and lake bottoms.

It's the same business, right? Wood? No: it's a horse of an entirely different color—felling big trees from forests as opposed to raising water-logged lumber.

The operations manager decides to accept a contract that could put the company on the map. He then passes the order down to field supervisors. They have no idea what these people are talking about, and say so.

They're told, "Figure it out."

So, they decide to do the best they can, holding out hope for success. Despite their efforts, the project ultimately fails, leaving a bad taste in the customer's mouth, creating infighting between departments, and lowering morale. This causes the beginning of a downward spiral in the company.

And it all happens because of poor decision-making, from top to bottom.

That story illustrates that blue-collar managers don't matter *any more or any less* than people in other levels of management. They are equally important because the *impact* of their decisions is the same as that of any other managers. The difference is in the power base. Had upper management really stopped and listened to the front line, the outcomes would have been different. Had there been conversations with understandings, success could have been achieved.

Some Say Blue-Collar People Can't Cut It as Managers

Some business owners and senior executives believe that blue-collar workers can't cut it as managers. They believe they don't have the necessary intelligence, can't learn, and would be better off sticking to being a wrench monkey. In prior experiences, they were disappointed because they promoted blue-collar workers to management and it did not work out. Therefore, they believe, it is better to leave blue-collar workers out of the ranks of management.

Or even worse: let's give them the *title* of manager, but in reality, they'll just be a messenger.

That is a gross miscalculation. These are the two main reasons why:

- First, when blue-collar workers are promoted to management, they are most frequently promoted without any preparation or training on how to actually manage. They are being set up for failure. No one likes to be set up to fail.
- The second reason for failure is the selection process for promotion. Typically, when a person is promoted from labor to management—or indeed at any level of management—it is because he was good at his job. But remember, that job—

working primarily with tools and objects—was very different than working with people and data, which is what management is (more on this later in the section "Selecting for Success").

When managers are not prepared for success, five areas begin to fail, and these have ultimately led to the downfall of entire companies. These failures are:

1. Low morale
2. Loss of productivity
3. Poor quality
4. Indifference to safety
5. Loss of intellectual capital (institutional knowledge) when people leave

Why did you leave the last company you worked for? Things like pay and benefits being equal, the decision to leave probably had a lot to do with the belief that the boss at the next job *might* be better than the old boss.

Maybe the previous boss wasn't good at being a boss—she didn't communicate, made poor decisions, didn't hold people accountable or was not accountable herself. Maybe she micromanaged; the list goes on. I'm not saying those are the only reasons people leave a company; I'm saying that a primary reason people start looking for and leaving jobs is a poor relationship with or view of someone there. People don't leave companies; people leave people. People leave bad bosses.

> *People don't leave companies; people leave people.*
> *People leave bad bosses.*

People stay where they feel valued, listened to, and where they have a sense of control over decisions that affect their work, lives, and futures. The person with the greatest influence on those things is their immediate supervisor. People are loyal to good bosses. That loyalty keeps them around through thick and thin, good times and bad. People like being around people who make good decisions, treat them fairly, and are concerned about the well-being of individuals and the team. When people are loyal to their bosses they will work more hours for less pay, stay when the ship is sinking, and work when conditions are far from ideal.

In an age where we are supposedly breaking down barriers in the workplace, we still fail in some areas. One of those areas is preparing, developing, and supporting blue-collar managers. We hire or promote them primarily because they are good technicians. They're good at what they do in the labor pool. And we promote them because we like them.

Without training and guidance, we are asking them to rewire their brains *without showing them the blueprints*. It's like asking a novice electrician to rewire the Empire State Building without giving him the blueprints—it's not going to end well.

When people are learning a new physical craft or skill—turning wrenches, pulling wire, driving a car and so on, their motor skills become more automated the more they do the job. Eye-hand coordination becomes stronger; decisions and actions are carried out almost without thought. When you first learned to drive a car, you were lucky to get out of the driveway, scared to make a left turn, and paralyzed by parallel parking. As time went on and you gained experience, driving became such a habit that you could arrive at work and not remember how you got there. The same thing happens when developing any new craft or skill. Hammering a nail, felling a tree, or dropping a building becomes second nature.

As time passes and experience grows, the eyes, ears, hands, and brain become quite skilled at sensing immediate feedback and correcting for changing conditions. But it wasn't so easy to begin with. It took time to learn and develop these skills. People watched, listened, questioned, tried and tried again until they got it right. Then they went a step further. The really good ones asked, "Why this way? Is there not a better way?" They thought about what they were doing and reasoned out why they did it that way. If it still made sense, they continued. If there was a better way, they adapted.

In short, their competencies came from observation, effort, asking questions, listening to stories, training—formal or informal—and just plain time and repetition doing the job.

When we hire people for a trade or craft, we can measure their competency with some degree of objectivity. We see their training certifications. We can directly observe how well they hammer a nail, tighten a bolt, drive a forklift, change out a pump, wire a house, fix the turbine on a jet engine, or drill an oil well. We can do this because we receive direct and instant feedback. We have baselines and expectations for measuring productivity.

But when we hire or promote someone to management or supervision, things are a little different. What are the benchmarks for success? How do you objectively measure a manager's or supervisor's production? It's a well-known fact that people rise to their level of incompetence. But how do you know whether they will be competent at the next level? How much time will you allow them to prove their competency? What can you do to help them? What will you do to help them overcome any incompetencies they have?

Businesses (and managers) that don't take the time to ask and answer those questions are more likely to end up with mediocre management at best. At worst, they'll end up with a messenger and not a manager.

The problem (beyond the obvious—having invested time, energy, and dollars into this person) is the fact that you will lose a valuable asset. The manager was promoted because he or she was good at something. The manager has knowledge and skills that can be transferred, and the ability to connect with a team in a way that someone without his or her knowledge wouldn't. Now the manager is gone, along with valuable institutional knowledge.

Everyone loses. Except, perhaps, your competition.

The real tragedy, though, is that you can extend and expand a blue-collar manager's competency with proper support and development. This is skill development, in much the same way as the development of the original craft. It is not just offering feedback; it means having a system to help new leaders understand their roles and responsibilities, and giving them the tools, time, and training to develop their new skills.

It means that they, and you, need to treat this next level in business as their new craft, their new trade. They are going to need help assembling their toolbox.

As best-selling author and mentor of mine, Jim Horan, has told me on several occasions, "The next level requires the next level of discipline." In the case of blue-collar managers and supervisors, regardless of their time in the position, whether they are new or have been around a while, they will need the next level of tools in their toolbox.

Remember Michael the pipe fitter turned manager? At risk of losing his management job after one year, he got some basic, but essential, training. Now, instead of a mediocre department manager at risk of losing his job, he is a regional manager for an area that covers a major portion of California.

We have these smart, hardworking people who want to do a great job. They want to make an impact. They want respect. Who doesn't want respect for the job they are doing?

Manager or Messenger?

Managers and supervisors come in all shapes and sizes, from all walks of life, experiences, and education. They are two ends of the same scale, and most fall somewhere in between. Some are blustery and charismatic with egos the size of the Great Wall of China—you can see them from outer space. They're hard-charging, devil-may-care, blustery, talk a big talk and sometimes walk that talk. On the other end of the scale are those who are quiet, humble, analytic, and/or unassuming.

On both ends of this scale and everywhere in between, some people chew other people up and spit them out, use them for their own purposes, and don't care about individuals. Their stats show high turnover rates and low morale.

Then there are those who fall somewhere along the scale, who may not be naturally good with people, but they know that people are the path to success in any endeavor. They know the value of their people, and so they work with them. They lead them. They manage data and lead people.

When a manager or supervisor is not a leader, he or she is a messenger. In one form or another, these kinds of managers merely relay the boss's or the company's policy to the crew, hoping the crew will perform and not shame them. This type of supervisor says things like, "The boss wants us to . . ." or "They said we have to . . ." or "Because I said so." None of those carry much weight in the long term. They diminish the managers' status, reducing them to mere messengers.

My point is this—the title is meaningless unless someone can lead people.

For the untrained manager or supervisor, promotion is soon seen as punishment.

A Word About Blue-Collar Women

I know this section is going to set some guys' teeth on edge, but get over it.

Men and women alike make up the blue-collar workforce, and since it's primarily a male-dominated arena, blue-collar women deserve a special word. I don't mean to separate women from the pack. Quite the contrary; it is my intent that women be respected and considered for training and promotion as much anyone else in the blue-collar community. In any community.

Women have a fight on their hands. It's not a matter of women having to prove their effectiveness and value in the workplace. It's a matter of men accepting it. It astonishes me that in this day and age, women's value continues to be an issue. The women I have worked with over the years are diligent, care for people (men, take note), are avid listeners and learners.

Years ago, I was in a grueling twelve-hour-a-day, three-day seminar that finished with an eight-hour exam. During the introduction on the first morning, one of the three instructors addressed the 200 of us in attendance with the following: "From a percentage standpoint, more women will pass this class with higher marks than the men. Know why? Because they are willing to set aside egos and admit that they don't know what they don't know, ask questions that others won't, study harder, and work at it for longer hours."

He was right forty years ago. And he is still right.

The women I have worked with over the span of my career have proven time and again to be as capable as any man.

Treat *all* people with respect. When considering a person for promotion or hiring new management, look at them as potential business partners. You might be amazed at how that attitude can open your eyes to hidden gems.

Why Working Supervisors Have Multiple Personalities

The working supervisor. *Sheesh.* In my experience, this is management purgatory and may well be hell on earth. Working supervisors sometimes seem to have split personalities—the Jekyll and Hyde of the workforce. They are good people being asked by *you* to have multiple personalities.

This is because we are asking them both to produce work and to lead people. This requires them to switch their brains between tasks and roles. As we've covered already, they are required to shift from working primarily with tools and objects to people and data, but these people have to do so frequently throughout the day.

Think about the times that you have been engrossed in something: writing a report, working on a spreadsheet, or participating in a sales meeting, and someone interrupted to tell you about a crisis with a client or coworker or at home. It was something so totally different than anything on your horizon that it took time to realize what they were talking about, and whether it was important to you and how to deal with it. Think about that feeling.

Confusion might have been mixed with disbelief and irritation that the person had the audacity to interrupt you. Then you got yourself under control, hopefully, and dealt with the situation. When that was done, you felt tired—maybe even exhausted. Think about how that felt. How it *still feels*.

Realize that is what you are asking a working supervisor to go through all day, every day: switching from one task and role to a different task and role and never getting their feet set. Never getting to do either task or role really well. How frustrating would that be for you?

The Peter Principle Is Still Right—But . . .

What got them there won't keep them there. Hiring or promoting blue-collar managers is most frequently based on their technical accomplishments. To be sure, they work with their peers to get things done. But life is different when working with peers and when former peers are now working for you.

The Peter Principle says people will rise to their level of incompetence. But is it really that they are incompetent? Or is it that they don't know what to do or how to do it? There is a difference. Just because you can't read or write doesn't mean you can't learn. You had to be taught. Training managers and supervisors can extend and expand their usefulness and their career, as well as save you time, frustration, and intellectual capital in the long run.

Training enhances competency and creates loyalty while adding to the bottom line.

Management Is Still a Craft

I'll repeat this like I vote—early and often: Blue-collar managers need to view their management roles as just as much a craft as their old roles. To excel at them, all crafts require training, mentoring, practice, and experience. Different crafts require different training and motivations. Successfully moving a person "off of the tools" and into management requires effort on everyone's part. It requires mental effort.

A goal without a process is like a comeback story without a struggle. It's empty. If the goal is to have a blue-collar worker become a successful manager, that requires a process as well, but it must be a flexible process. The goal is to rewire the new manager's brain. The process is much more than just giving someone a title. Fortunately, it doesn't require brain surgery.

A bad manager can take a good team and destroy it.

A good manager will take a team and develop it, sparking innovation, increasing productivity, enhancing safety, raising morale, and instilling loyalty.

When Should You Train?

Now.

Start training now.

A great time to start is before you actually promote people. Just like their old trade, make them apprentices in this new trade.

A great place to start is with the notebook method.

If you are waiting for the planets to align and all of your employees to be ready at the same time, it will be too late. No two people grow in the same direction at the same pace. This includes your managers and supervisors. So, waiting for them to get ready and hoping they will be able to keep pace is fruitless. Make your training program flexible, adaptable, user-friendly.

If your concern is the economy, don't let it be. In an economic downturn, training gets set aside. People say that funds aren't available. Apparently, though, funds are always available to clean up the mess left behind by an incompetent manager. You use nonexistent funds to find a replacement manager. And another. And another. Alternatively, you can keep the managers you have, develop them into the people you want, and create loyalty and productivity along the way.

Customer loyalty is fickle. Training in an economic downturn is even more critical. Smart business people don't compete on pricing alone, but in a down economy, customers tend to shop pricing more than usual. Separate your business from the competition. Give better customer service, deliver ahead of schedule, and deliver higher quality. Be consistent. You do this through more efficient processes, which require good planning and decision-making. You do this, ultimately, through your people.

What about training when the times are good? In a booming economy, the available pool of competent people in the workforce is drastically diminished. All of the good people are already at work, and it's going to cost you a premium to snag one of them. Or you can create great people of your own who are familiar with your business, and because you show you care enough about them to train and mentor them, they become even more loyal.

Some industries, such as oil and gas, are trending toward keeping older, more experienced workers instead of just replacing them with younger people who have less experience. Their leaders learned this lesson from previous slumps in the industry when experienced people left and changed careers in order to survive. This left a large deficit in the knowledge bank—brain-drain.

The result in the oil and gas industry was that when the economy turned around, there weren't enough experienced people available in what is arguably one of the toughest industries to maintain. They now recognize the value of retaining experienced people to mentor those with less experience.

When you lose people, especially those with experience, the sticker price isn't the total cost. By sticker price, I mean their salaries and the cost of advertising for replacements. The true cost of replacement can add up to (depending on the source you subscribe to) anywhere from three to fifteen times a person's salary. But there's more. What if the person who left causes or had caused the loss of more than one person?

What if they caused the loss of your top client?

It happens. And it's not pretty.

When you lose good people, you:

- lose institutional knowledge and intellectual capital
- create a downward spiral in confidence and morale
- now have to manage mediocrity

If you aren't developing your people, you're making your competition's case against you.

Which Sounds Best? To Be Mediocre or To Be a Force Multiplier?

Processes and procedures are great, but they can also have their pitfalls. Rigid processes support formulaic decision-making and destroy creative thinking. When it comes to developing people, rigid processes can create mediocrity. People begin to think that good enough is, well, *good enough*. This is when you hear, "It's not in my job description."

Instead of looking at training as a necessary evil, look at it as the opportunity to bring out the potential in people. If you teach a person how to be a manager in the truest sense, then by default, you develop more people. You develop the people who work with the trained manager. That little bit of encouragement and mentoring is a force multiplier—that one person can instill growth in several others, which in turn instills growth in even more people.

- Teach your managers and supervisors that, regardless of their title, they lead people, manage numbers and data, and solve problems.
- Watch for signs that current blue-collar leaders are messengers and not managers. Evaluate why

that is happening. Is it your style that is causing that? Or something else?

- Remember that typically people are promoted because they were good at doing something technical and because they were well liked. Those are not determining factors in future success. They help, but they don't guarantee success.

›LESSON 3‹

They Don't Talk About Management By Gunpoint

Not one single management or leadership author I have ever read talks about management by gunpoint. Not Kotter, not Cohen, and not John Maxwell.

My first encounter with management by gunpoint was in South Texas, near Laredo, in December of 1981. Fortunately, it was also my last involvement.

We were drilling a wildcat oil well on a ranch 100 miles from nowhere, and the rig was thirteen miles from the nearest paved road. Everything that lived there had horns, thorns, or teeth. If you walked cross-country, though, you wound your way through cactus, longhorns, and rattlers. Trucks and bulldozers had turned the hard, sunbaked clay into dust that was boot-top deep.

When the rains came, that dust was churned into mud. Knee-deep, boot-sucking, gooey mud. And then, unless you were lucky enough to catch a ride on a dozer, you had to walk the last three miles. You couldn't walk along the road, as the ruts were almost hip-deep, like walking in a canyon with mud walls.

When the well had reached total depth, and we determined it was viable, the next step was getting the well ready for production. This meant running pipe, an operation that involved inserting steel pipe the size of a small sewer main to a depth of nearly two miles. The weather had been nasty for days. Desolate, gray, rainy skies for days on end, bitterly cold nights that cut to the bone. The day became night and night became day seamlessly, with no change in light or dark. Then ice and sleet started. The rig floor was slick with mud and attempts to wash it off just left another layer of ice. Icicles hung from the derrick as if waiting for the chance to fall and impale a man. There are many hells in life, and this was one of them.

On this day, the crew that worked graveyard didn't show up. Evening shift had to double over to cover. Then the next shift didn't show, causing the same crew to stay yet again, almost 24 hours total. We had battled the elements for weeks on what would normally be a one-week job. We were within sight of going home. You do whatever it takes to get the job done.

The roughnecks were exhausted and with icy mud underfoot and ice daggers overhead, this wasn't going to be a safe or easy operation. The first clue that something was wrong was when the rhythm of the rig changed. Drilling rigs have a heartbeat of their own, and you can feel it and hear it in the motors and other equipment. Something had changed. The big diesel motors had slowed and stayed idle for much longer than normal.

Stairs covered in black ice led to the doghouse—the metal shack up off of the edge of the floor where the crew might be taking a break. It was empty. No one there. The crew was nowhere to be found. The crew had walked off of the job and out into the scrub brush and cactus in a long, sweeping, miserable, muddy arc in order to not be seen on the way to their vehicles.

When they got to their trucks, someone was waiting for them.

They were, soaked, freezing, and hungry. They didn't have much fight left in them. Nothing much was said as they stood in the rain and sleet. It was pointed out that they had to get back and complete the job or all was lost.

They argued a little. A gun was drawn.

A six-gun is an argument killer—you don't draw a gun unless you intend to use it. The dejected crew went back to work and did the job grudgingly. But they got it done.

That crew deserves an apology. All anyone knew about work ethic at the time was that you got the job done, whatever it took. What people didn't understand, but we've come to realize and study, is that people's needs are different, people's motivations are different, and that just because someone has the title of "boss," that didn't make him one.

Retired four-star Marine General Anthony Zinni, decorated war veteran and former head of the U.S. Forces Central Command, learned early on that we could win all the battles in the world, but in order to create true and lasting change, we have to win people's hearts and minds.

The battles are no different in corporate America. As leaders and managers, when we don't win their hearts and nourish their minds, we don't create change. We just leave devastation in our wake.

You might think, "Interesting story, but that would never happen today, and for sure not in my organization," to which I'll have to throw the bullsh*t flag. Why? Because today's managers use a different kind of gun. The ways we have figured out to threaten people into doing their jobs are astounding. We threaten people with time off, loss of pay, loss of job, loss of the corner office, loss of the employee parking spot, loss of something.

We shame people.

These are different threats, but just as effective as a gun.

Threats mean we intend to harm people. When we threaten people, we are saying we intend to take something away, whether it is their lives or their livelihoods. Whether or not that threat is ever carried out, the act itself has reduced or removed three of the primary driving forces that all humans have—the need for respect, security, and hope for the future.

You can develop a deeper understanding of the basics of human wants, needs, and behaviors. You can begin to do this by treating your own position as a craft. Start to understand how and why people do things, even if it's at a very high level. Study your craft. Study people and what makes them effective, ineffective, and how you can help them. Really own the fact that people don't act the way you act, think the way you think, and do things for the same reasons you do. Know that they are probably not motivated by the same things you are.

Never assume that the managers you manage know how to do something. I'm not talking about assuming they are stupid, or that they need micromanagement, or that they should describe every detail of what they are about to do before you let them do it. I'm saying that especially in the world of management, no matter the level, be observant and cognizant of their abilities and be willing to offer help and guidance when you can.

There's a phrase in the world of training: *The curse of knowledge*. It means that since *we* know something, *they* should know it. Knowledge doesn't work that way.

›LESSON 4‹

The Underpinning of Management and Leadership—Communication

Of all of the areas in which you can possibly choose to help your managers grow and become more effective, communication is at the very top.

There was a stand of tall trees bordering an airfield in the Midwest. The county supervisor told the maintenance crew to cut down half of the trees.

The expectation:

The results:

This demonstrates the need for precision when managing and leading people. Don't assume that the recipient should know what you mean. (Remember, when the word "should" is involved, prepare to be disappointed.) My point is that, after trust, communication is more powerful than anything in business. You don't have to go any further than the latest headlines to see where the power of communication lies.

The Definition of Communication Is Incomplete

Whenever I prepare a seminar on leadership, I look up the definition of communication. In all the years I have been doing this, websites tell me that the word communication is in the top 1 percent of searches. Why do you think that is?

Definitions of the word communication include:

- "An act or instance of transmitting," followed by "information communicated" (I am curious why the word being defined is included in the definition itself)
- "Information transmitted or conveyed"

Continue to read definitions of communication, and you will find words like "process," "act," "exchange," "system," "technique," and so forth. So, what is missing?

In a word? *Understanding*.

Delivered does not mean *received*, and *received* does not mean *understood*. An example is the use of email programs. As the sender, you have the option to ask for both a delivery receipt and a read receipt. The implication is that your job is done when you get a delivery receipt, and at that point, your butt is covered. If you get a read receipt, well, surely the recipients did, in fact, open the message, and read the email, and understood it, or they would reply. Right?

No. Neither is true. There is no understood receipt when sending an email.

It's like when you buy something online, and you aren't around when UPS comes by. You get a text that says the package was delivered. But you have not personally received the package, opened it, or taken the product out and read the instructions and used it satisfactorily.

Let me be clear here: Real communication must include understanding.

We want to create understanding, because only then can the correct action happen—actions that include such things as meeting goals, being efficient, and working safely.

What Causes Misunderstanding?

Misunderstanding happens because of:

- **Different communication (behavioral) styles.** People often transmit information with a different style than the recipient prefers to receive it.
- **Different learning styles.** If a person is a visual and kinesthetic learner, then the notebook is an

even better tool for communicating with him. (It's actually better for every learning style, as the act of writing helps cement learning in the brain.)

- **Distractions that take people's attention away from the message.** Things like text messages, emails, road traffic, work going on in the vicinity, bright shiny objects, high noise areas, etc. can interfere with understanding.
- **Unintentional distrust.** If there is distrust, the listeners' understanding can be blocked by thoughts that perhaps the manager is setting them up for failure, wondering what the manager isn't saying, etc. They aren't focused on the message.
- **Intentional (subversive) distrust.** If a manager and employees have a serious break in their relationship, the employees may purposefully look for unclear communication and act in a subversive way.
- **The words you choose.** Poor grammar or overuse of jargon can lead to lost meaning or disagreement about what a word or phrase means, and industry jargon can get in the way.

Why don't people admit they don't understand? The most common reasons are:

- **They don't want to appear to be ignorant or foolish.** They think the admission makes them look weak and they are ashamed of it.

- **They are distrustful.** They fear it is not safe to speak up because they think they are going to get shamed.

- **They don't have the confidence to speak up.** For all of the above reasons as well as their own behavioral style, the quiet introvert is less likely to speak up for fear of drawing attention to him or herself.

Ultimately, it's the fear of shame that causes people to remain silent.

No, They Really Weren't Born to Piss You Off

We all know a person we think was born just to piss us off. You know the one—dealing with him (or her) is like chewing on aluminum foil. In fact, that person may think the same of you. But you really weren't born to piss each other off. Here's why.

We humans judge people initially on their physical appearance. It is what it is. We do it, and if we think we want to develop a relationship deeper than just blowing them off, we learn to see past their style of dress or other physical appearances. The one area that is tough to overlook is behavior. It is behavior that we either love, hate, or don't care about. When a person does things in a manner that leaves you grimacing and thinking, "I would never act that way!" it irks us. It feels like they're standing on our last nerve. But remember, behavior is *how* people do things.

Take a moment and think about *that person*. Bring an image to mind and see if you can determine what it is that irks you. Is it how the person dresses, walks, or talks? Is it how that person solves problems, influences others, resists change, and pays attention to the rules? When people don't behave according to our personal ideals, then they irritate us. When they don't do things the way we would do them, that really gets to us.

Behavior—How People Do Things

Without rewriting the textbook on behavior, let's just look at the basics.

Each one of the following characteristics exists on a sliding scale. Some people can be found at the extreme ends of the scale, but usually, people are somewhere in between.

Caution: Just because people may fall at the extremes does not make them good or bad people. It doesn't even make them good or bad employees. As we'll see later in Selecting for Success, the characteristics of their behavior can make them a better fit for the job.

- **How people attack problems:** On one end of the scale, we have the intuitive and decisive person who can make snap decisions very quickly. On the other end, we have those who are deliberate, gather the data they need, and evaluate all their options before making a decision.

- **How people influence others**: One end of the scale is the chatty, "I'm here! Where's the party?" person, and on the other, the quiet introvert, not always speaking up because it can be difficult. Introverts keep to themselves and wait for things to happen or for others to notice them.
- **People resist change, and this can be a good thing or not.** It depends on the job we need them to do. At one end, we have people who will go anywhere and do anything at the drop of a hat, and they'll drop that hat themselves. At the other end, we have people who show up at the same place at the same time and do the same job every day for their entire career, and they actually prefer that.
- **Then there are rules.** Yes. Rules. Some people work on the premise that rules are good. But rules are for others, aren't they? The other end of that scale believes rules exist for a purpose and everyone must follow them in every situation (think DMV here).

It is worth noting that behavior can change situationally, but our natural behavioral style preferences are always just beneath the surface. With respect to communication, I am an advocate of changing behavior in the moment—not to manipulate someone, but rather to help the listener understand what is being transmitted. Changing behavioral style during communication is the equivalent of changing languages for the purpose of a conversation. When you shift to speaking to someone in their native tongue, they more readily understand you and are more willing to hear you.

How Behavior Affects Communication

Pipeline service company owner: "I know they're gonna be mad at me, but let's do that email changeover you talked about."

Manager: "Who is going to be mad at you and why?"

Owner: "The other managers and that other IT guy. They've been trying to get me to change how we have our email set up on the internet for years. I know it's caused problems, but now I know what that change does for us. They're going to be mad because I listened to you and not them."

Manager: "Why did you listen to me?"

Owner: "Because you said it differently. You said it where I could understand it. You didn't use a five-dollar word when a fifty-cent word would do. You gave me the bottom line up front, then you gave me a short list of the items that would affect us most. I didn't need to know how the internet worked, or how a mail server works like those other guys kept telling me."

That was a dialogue between a company owner and a manager who understood that the need to change the company's email system was critical. He *had* to try a different way to get the point across to the owner. Past approaches hadn't worked.

Having dealt with the owner successfully on other matters, he was able to shift the manager's thinking in terms of behavior. While the owner was talking about the *words* the manager was using, in truth it was the *behavior style* that affected the words the manager used.

Since behavior is really about *how* people do things, it has a lot of influence on how people communicate. Mismatched behavior causes misunderstanding because of a mismatch in communication styles. Think about how you like to receive information and how your managers deliver it. Then think about how they communicate and how that affects the way they receive information.

In general, people communicate in one of four different ways. I like to use the spreadsheet as an example. Everyone knows about spreadsheets. Here are how the four different styles of communicators view the spreadsheet:

1. **Bob the bottom-liner.** "What's the bottom line? I know about the spreadsheet. Put it on my desk. I'll look at it later. Maybe."
2. **Isabela the influential.** "Hey! What's happenin'? Are you going to the party? Maybe we can chat a little over a drink? How about those guys moving their team away from here? Did you see that latest tip about how the straps on your shoes need to line up with the central line of your leg? Oh, yeah, listen, I have this idea, and, well, it'd be really

cool if you could look at it. I kinda thought about it and well..." (Isabela and Chatty Cathy get along great.)

3. **Simon the sage.** The steady, supportive person, Simon knows that somewhere out there is this thing called a spreadsheet. He may or may not have ever seen one, but he does know this: the spreadsheet knows all and holds all of the rules. His quiet advice would be to look at the spreadsheet and see if it had any good suggestions to follow.

4. **Abby the analytic.** Abby is the creator and holder of the spreadsheet. When she does actually communicate, it is typically with too much information for the other styles. She starts her approach with an email and spreadsheet attached. The email tells you why there is a spreadsheet, describes how the spreadsheet was developed, and even goes so far as to tell you...*grrrr*...to get to the bottom line, you have to actually open the spreadsheet and scan it!

With a little thought, you can probably recognize yourself and others in the above behavior styles. Those examples demonstrate the extremes. Most people are a blend of two or more. So, don't you just love it when the analytic mechanic gets really chatty about how he discovered the fuel blockage and it wasn't actually the filter, but rather an air bubble in the injector system, and all you wanted to know is whether the truck is running?

Behavior affects communication, and it is helpful here to use assessments so people can read about how their natural preferred style works for or against them. Natural behavior is also fairly well fixed in a person. People can and do adapt for long periods of time, but that ends up hurting them physically and emotionally. So, I don't ask people to change who they are at their core. I ask them to adapt in the moment to their audience's behavioral style so that the message can be understood.

When you observe people long enough, or perhaps if you've read behavioral assessments about them, you can see temporary shifts in their behavior. Some of this is good. In fact, it's great if someone shifts when communicating with a person with a different communication style. For instance, a Bob the Bottom-line type manager doesn't feel the need to explain himself. Then he has to report to Abby the Analytic, who requires *all* of the information in a neat and orderly package so that she can see whether Bob got to the bottom line the way she would.

Think ex-merchant marine or former longshoreman talking to the head of the accounting department: a mismatch made in heaven (or the other place) if there ever was one. Work with Mike the marine or Larry the longshoreman to temporarily adapt their behavior, which will affect communication. Get them to string together a few bullet points with details and the accountant will more readily accept working with them. Similarly, if the accountant would just get to the point, or the bottom line, then the longshoreman and the merchant marine will appreciate it. They don't want the details to start with. They'll ask if they want them. While this example may seem extreme, it serves to point out potential conflict in communication.

Working with a former Navy petty officer now in charge of mechanics in civilian life, we had an issue that kept understanding at bay. When asked a question, Mario would always answer, "Joe knows!" Joe was the boss two levels above Mario. And Joe frequently *didn't* know. We had to gently apply pressure, questions, and use humor, and yes, it got a little uncomfortable at times, but with gentle nudging, Mario eventually gave up the information. Mario wasn't naturally given to explanations or detail. His immediate superior, Arno, was highly analytic and always had notes with bullet points. Mario simply used "Joe knows!" to avoid having to deal with Arno.

Misunderstanding Can Kill

A misunderstanding that once occurred on a pipeline construction job highlights the potential impact on safety and could have resulted in the death of an employee.

Jason's head was a foot away from the trap door on a pipeline when it blew open and nearly decapitated him. The door weighed half as much as a Chevy Spark, with the trajectory of a flat-nosed bullet. Jason was part of a crew cleaning out a pipeline using a method called pigging. Foam or rubber plugs are inserted into the line via a launcher and recovered using a receiver. The receiver has a trap door that opens to pull the pig out.

After it was launched, this pig was pushed with compressed air, and though it was only traveling at three or four miles per hour, the pig develops a lot of energy. Imagine a hard, foam and rubber bullet bigger than your barbecue grill's propane bottle. When it hit the end of the line, it blew the trap door off of the receiver and passed within inches of the employee's head.

Working with the supervisor and others on the safety committee, we introduced a method for communication on operations like these that reduces the potential for error. It's a direct feedback system. Someone sends a message that is very simple, yet very specific. The recipient repeats the message back to the sender exactly the way it was received and asks for any clarification or additional information if he needs it. If the receiver doesn't send back the appropriate message, the sender stops operations until the situation is clarified.

It works an awful lot like the way we're taught to listen during a critical conversation, right?

The Big Myth about the Words We Use

In 1971, Albert Mehrabian published the results of a study that the media and communication gurus subsequently misinterpreted and repeated. This disservice resulted in a myth that has become a mainstay of communication, in gross disservice to people trying to communicate effectively.

The study was purported to reveal that 55 percent of communication is body language, 38 percent is tone of voice, and 7 percent is the words you use. If you were to look at summaries of the actual study, however, it is evident that Mehrabian was talking about communication within a very narrow frame: When body language doesn't match the words being spoken, people tend to believe the body language.

Words matter. This is especially true when all you have to interpret is the text of an email, memo, or text message, because in those cases, *all you have are words.*

Choose your words wisely. Read *their* words for understanding. Teach your managers and supervisors to choose their words wisely and to be specific.

When working with blue-collar people, indeed with anybody, whether they are in management or still on the tools, the most critical thing in communication is respect. Always show them respect, even when they don't return it. They will eventually.

Help them to understand that the words they use and their tone of voice are significant. Grunting and chin-pointing don't get the job done. Remind them that they and their team are more than likely visual as well as kinesthetic learners, and it is possible that the move to management has shifted the way they view their team members. They may have forgotten that things like a clear understanding of *what* and *why* they were asked to do something were once important to them, and they remain important to the people on their team.

Voice and body language add effect to words. They cannot *replace* the words. They can, in some instances, add humor or emotion to the words. But the words carry the message.

What You Can Do

Near the middle of my career as a manager, the work that I loved seemed like it was getting more difficult. Not the technical side of it; the people side. I just wanted them to give me the problem and get the hell out of my way while I fixed it. Silly people, thinking I wanted their help. But the stress was mounting.

At the age of thirty-eight, I ended up in a hospital emergency room because they thought I had suffered a heart attack. At that time, I was working eighteen-hour days, drinking a pot of coffee every morning, two liters of soda every afternoon, and smoking two packs of cigarettes every day. One morning I got the bright idea to quit it all; the smoking, coffee, and sodas, all at once. *BAM!* Cold turkey!

When I walked into my office the next morning my crew and my boss were gathered in there, waiting for me. The following items were on my desk—a hot cup of coffee, a pack of cigarettes and a lighter, a clean ashtray, and a copy of the book *How to Win Friends and Influence People*. My boss looked at me, shook his head, said, "No more," and then they all walked out.

I know a hint when I'm hit over the head with it. I was in trouble, not because of my technical skills, but because of my people skills. Or lack of them. Communication was the key.

Here are some things you can do to help your managers become better communicators.

First, get to know *their* communication style, both in a relaxed environment and under stress. Knowing both is critical to knowing how they will act or react in different circumstances. Do this by having conversations with them, and not just when something is critical. Make a point of seeking them out and learning more about them, about their lives. Listen to their stories, and you'll begin to understand not only how they communicate, but how they think.

Second, begin to adapt your communication style to theirs in the moments when you are dealing with them, so that they more readily receive information from you. Over time, this will also help develop trust between you.

Third, each of you should answer the questions on the "Can't We Just Get Along?" form.[1] Share the results with each other. Ask them to share the results with their teams. If you think it would be valuable, I highly recommend that each of the direct reports answers the questions as well.

Fourth, as their manager, remember that you are also their coach and mentor—and referee. Help them get better at recognizing and understanding how to communicate with the other various styles.

---

[1] The link to this download is found in the "Resources" section of this book.

Fifth, when in a meeting with others who use various communication styles, tell everyone well in advance that when it is their turn to talk about their department, they can help facilitate communication by starting with one of the following phrases:

- The bottom line is...and here is why...
- The point I would like to discuss is...and here is why...
- The problem I need help with is...and here is why...
- The opportunity we have is...and here is why...

You can come up with any number of other phrases to start the conversation in a meeting, but they must focus on the issue at hand from the outset. Then and only then can people go into the story or details.

Some final thoughts:

- Conversations are a great way to communicate to understand.
- Conversations become easier the more they happen.
- Constant communication about smaller issues build trust and make it easier to have a conversation about the bigger issues when they come up.
- Smaller issues are likely the cause of the bigger issue, so having regular conversations will reduce the likelihood of the bigger issue happening.

- If you want them to change, you will have to change first. You will have to adapt your communication style to meet theirs before they will be willing to adapt theirs to yours.

› LESSON 5 ‹

The Keys to Success are Rarely in a Job Description

Key accountabilities are the measurable objectives of a position. These are not mere tasks. They *do not address* timeliness, vacation, sick days, etc. They address real work. These are the essence of the job, the critical goals to be met that make the job and team a success.

What does the *position* need to achieve so that the business unit is successful? How can we measure that over time? Notice the focus on the position, rather than the person, at first. This is because otherwise, we tend to look at a position and have a person in mind to fill it, then we begin to make allowances for them, thinking they may be incapable of doing all of the critical tasks required. So, we never set the criteria, and then we (and they) are disappointed when the nonexistent criteria aren't met. Remember Michael's story?

Here are some very real examples of key accountabilities:

- Build twelve miles of twenty-four-inch pipeline in four months.

- Reduce turnover from 25 percent to 5 percent in the next twelve months.
- Train 100 percent of the team on OSHA's Focus Four.
- Have key documentation (name it) completed on time, 100 percent of the time.

Most of my work involves people who don't have a clear picture of what they are required to do, no objective way of measuring whether they are on the right track, and who feel like they have no input into the process. Often, I hear that a manager is in trouble, and her manager wants a way to make sure she damn well understands what is required of her. The bosses want what is commonly referred to as a Performance Improvement Plan. This is usually the last straw before the one in trouble gets fired.

What I am always curious about is why the *last* thing done to save the employee is to be absolutely clear on the expectations. Why isn't that the *first* thing that is done? Why don't the managers stop and think about what they really want from employees and let them know those criteria beforehand?

Being clear on expectations requires effort. It takes thought. For this process to work, you have to spend some time thinking, writing, and talking, then writing some more.

Sometimes managers aren't clear on expectations because they don't know how to be.

Here's a great way to start: Have a conversation with your manager. Come to an agreement on what the job requires. If you haven't filled a position, even better. Talk to people who previously worked in that position. Talk to the people who work in concert with that position—coworkers, peers, and employees who report to the person in that position. Talk to the people who need something from that position—like reports, paperwork, logistics, supplies, scheduling, whatever. Ask them: "What does the *position* need to do for you so that you get your job done in an efficient manner?" Don't let them focus on the person, yet.

The typical job description doesn't include these requirements in any meaningful way. I won't bore you with a rant about how job descriptions don't typically help the hiring manager or the candidates understand what is truly required. Well, maybe a mini-rant.

Job descriptions usually begin by extolling the virtues of the company then end with "and anything else the company requires of you." Using a phrase like that means that the people who wrote it don't understand the job and think they need a *Hail Mary* phrase to cover anything and everything. And they really, really don't understand the unintended abuses that this phrase encourages. It means they don't care. There are many examples of managers using this term to make employees do the most embarrassing things, just to show control. Now, please go get your boss's dry cleaning and bring him a latte; I'm sorry you think you have a machine to repair.

But I digress.

Job descriptions, especially in the recruiting or hiring stage, include statements like "long hours, lots of travel, able to lift locomotives and leap tall buildings," etc., followed by a list of transferable skills—things like "familiar with MS Office, reading, writing, and arithmetic." Yes, these are critical to success, and yes, you need to pay attention to these.

But what does somebody need to focus on, objectively, to make that position a success?

Agreements Create Accountability

"Fire him."

"Let's not traumatize the guy. He's young and just needs to learn a tough lesson. We could just lay him off and avoid a lot of drama."

"How about we exercise the at-will clause? We can simply say, 'At will and without cause, we are severing our relationship.'"

"Wait. Why are we talking about this? Did he repeatedly violate written policy? Has he been counseled?"

My clients were having a discussion about whether to fire a young man and, if so, how to do it. There were those who advocated just laying him off. There were those who inquired about the reasons for firing him. Were the infractions and other reasons documented? No, there was no documentation. Then someone came up with the bright idea that they use the at-will clause; this wording would not give the released person anything to sue over. He'd just be gone.

Or, they finally said, we could do a Performance Improvement Program.

I asked them, "What does your Performance improvement program include?"

"Specific tasks, goals. and objectives."

"Are they measurable? Are they time sensitive?" (That's why they're called objectives, you know.)

Blank stares. "Yes. Maybe. I don't know."

"Have you given him these measurable criteria before, like, say, when he started the position?"

More blank stares. No eye contact. Papers were shuffled. Throats were cleared.

"Why do you wait until people are in trouble to be clear on what is required of them?

"It's in their job description."

Apparently not.

I have asked more than 150 people from labor to upper management the following question: "What is it about this place [their work] that pisses you off?" And 100 percent of the time, they bring up lack of accountability. They want people to be held accountable. They want to be held accountable. Being held personally accountable means that *you* know what *they* are doing. They want to know that you approve of what they are doing.

Believe it or not, most often, management is the group that doesn't want accountability. Why? Because accountability is a headache. The excuses I have heard over time include:

- They don't want a process that can be abused.
- They don't want the paperwork.
- They don't have time to hold people accountable.

People don't like to hold one another accountable. It's messy. It's stressful. It can be painful. We don't want to hurt someone's feelings. But let's just admit that the root cause of not holding people accountable is fear. The fear is that you'll be seen as a hard-ass, or that you will create conflict, or they won't respect you anymore.

The concern about a process that can be abused is legitimate. The concern is that a manager might take the process and run with it, "talking" to people and documenting it, writing them up, getting to the three-strikes-you're-out mode without thinking through the consequences. Fair enough. That just means you have to mentor managers, teach them how to make decisions. Which means you have to let them think. (I think I've said that before.)

You don't want the paperwork? I get that. I don't like paperwork any more than you do. But it's how the world, and attorneys, and management, works.

Why don't we talk about paperwork reduction by *preventing* the need for corrective or punitive action?

Accountability Requires Agreement

Accountability begins with *clarity*. If managers don't understand what goals the position needs to reach in order to be successful, they'll come up with their own. They won't be *your* goals, I assure you. Ask yourself, "Would I send an electrician out to wire an office without giving her the blueprints?" As managers, they are in positions of greater impact. Why would you not give them a blueprint, a vision, clarity of focus? They *want* to know what you want done, how you will measure success, how you agree to get the work done, and the tasks or projects required to be successful.

Accountability requires *objective measurement*. It's easier to hold a machinist accountable for making a part out of tolerance, or a dozer operator for not leveling the road to spec than it is to set objective measurements for a manager. It's only easier because someone took the time to think about what a job well done actually looks like.

Your key accountabilities document is the beginning of the blueprint for the manager's position. You, and they, just have to sit down and agree on the reasonable, measurable objectives to be used.

Some measurements will be absolute—build ten rock crushers. Some measurements will be relative—build more rock crushers than the other guy. But to be meaningful, they *will be measurable*. Like any venture in the blue-collar arena, nothing is exact. So, it's not a bad idea to come up with a tolerance. Like grading a slope to +/- 0.5 percent, there can be tolerances for your manager's performance. If you are concerned about them hitting the low mark, fine, but of the managers that I have worked with, the ones who took pride in their work swung for the high mark. That tolerance range can itself be an indicator of engagement.

Accountability requires *agreement*. People want to have some control over the decisions that affect their lives. They want to have input. This is the power of an agreement. When you get real input into people's job requirements, *from those people*, they feel heard, understood, and feel a sense of control. Don't get input just to go through the motions. Get input so that people feel they are part of the process. So they'll feel respected.

When you think you've reached an agreement on key accountabilities, shake hands and ask, "Do we have an agreement?" When they respond in the affirmative, then you have power built into this thing. This power—the power to say "I thought we had an agreement"—makes it easier to decide to hold someone accountable and then to actually do so.

Accountability requires agreement.
Agreement and accountability foster respect.

Scrapping the Annual Review Makes Accountability Easier

No one likes surprises, even good ones, and especially when the annual review comes around. Everyone hates each other's guts just before and on that one day of the year. The anticipation itself is enough to give an elephant a heart attack. It gets even better when you get a memo from your boss saying, "Yo! Yo! What up? It's that time of year! Let's meet and greet and get this thing done, but before we do, how about you rate yourself in the following areas? Does 8:00 a.m. Monday work for you?"

Um. No. No, not really.

So, scrap the annual review.

Here's how: Do the review monthly.

Pull the agreement out, sit down with the manager on a scheduled—monthly—basis, and have a discussion about what's working, what isn't, and what you both agree needs to be done moving forward. Never, ever, reschedule that conversation. Ever.

⟩ LESSON 6 ⟨

The Road to Success is Paved with Indecisive Squirrels

Drilling Down on Decision-Making

Imagine that you had to drill a hole in Mother Earth the diameter of a five-gallon bucket. At a mile straight down, you then start drilling a hole the size of a one-gallon bucket, but this time curving the hole to a thirty-degree angle in a specific direction. At about two miles down (that's 10,500 feet) you have to line that new hole with pipe, all the way back to the surface. That pipe will contain the flow of natural gas from that well.

It was Christmas of 1979 on the banks of the Trinity River near Anahuac, Texas. We had been drilling a gas well with a target zone out under the river. We had to drill a "slant-hole," drill at an angle, from the banks of the river, to get under it.

To this day I cannot pinpoint exactly where the problems started, but I can tell you what compounded the problems and ultimately cost the customer many hundreds of thousands of dollars: his decision-making process.

Things were going along just fine until Murphy's Law was invoked. There were a series of small and not-so-small misfortunes along the way, as often happens when working with Mother Earth. But the well was drilled successfully, and we went into the completion phase.

It was then that things really began to go sideways, no pun intended. The well kept trying to blow out; pipe kept getting stuck in the hole; the formation was spitting out gas, water, and sand, screwing up equipment, and so forth. It was at this point that the customer's senior engineer got involved in the decision-making process—one of the reasons I run when I hear the words "I'm from corporate, and I'm here to help."

There were four consultants, each with a specialty, but with a combined total of more than seventy years' experience, all backed by our boss, who had forty years' experience himself. We were constantly looking at data, feeling and sensing the movement of pipe, using experience and intuition to revise our game plan as needed. Each morning we called in the technical information to the client's engineer, so that he had the information we had. *Technically.*

But he didn't have two things we had—experience and the sense, the *feel*, of what was going on, because we could subconsciously compare the signs and symptoms from the well with our past experience on other projects. And we could visualize what was going on downhole.

The real problems began when the engineer asked for our recommendations, at which point he almost always decided to take another path—usually one we had thought of and had discarded. It got to the point where the stress was so bad, people were feeling physically ill. One of my fellow consultants, Jaime, was under so much stress that he contracted pneumonia. He found an old sawbones in the little town near us and got a penicillin shot every day for two weeks—that's a different discussion on decisions for another day.

One day, we were all gathered around the phone, about to call in our reports and recommendations, and I asked what the consensus was. Did we all agree to go with Option A and not Option B? Heads nodded. "Yes." I took the phone, got the engineer on the line, and gave him our reports and recommendations. This time, though, I told him, "We recommend Option B." The other consultants' jaws dropped as they leaped out of their chairs and started towards me. Fortunately, before they got to me, I got an answer from the engineer: "No. Go with Option A." I confirmed this, then hung up the phone and told the others the results.

The results were a success.

It doesn't matter how complex a decision is.
It doesn't matter at what level within the organization a decision is made.
What matters most is the impact of the results of the decision.

Decisions aren't made in vacuums. Decisions affect production, morale, safety, peers, the customer, and the bottom line. Making proper decisions, good decisions, means being engaged and willing to make those decisions. It also means being willing to risk making the wrong decision.

Indecision is a decision. It's a decision to ignore the issue at hand for any of a number of reasons, chief among which are the desire for the issue to just go away, and the fact that so many people don't know how to make good decisions.

What Are Good Decisions?

What makes a good decision? I ask because most people don't think about what constitutes a good decision. They just go with what feels right or what they think is right. Most people have no benchmark for what a good decision is. They have no criteria for making good decisions. That works right up until the results aren't what was expected. Then the questioning begins: "Why did you do that? What made you think that was the right way to do that?" and so forth.

A little FYI here: "It seemed like a good idea at the time" isn't the answer you are looking for.

Dealing with the Emotions of Decision-Making

Over the years, I have heard time and again that successful people remove emotion from decision-making. I throw the bullsh*t flag once again. I've been around many, many successful people, and I'll tell you this—the successful and creative people *start* the decision-making process based on an emotion. Perhaps the most common decision is, "Fire that S.O.B! He's not doing what he's supposed to." How many times have you heard, said, or thought that phrase? How did you act on it? *Emotionally?*

The best way to deal with emotions is to recognize them. Actually getting people to verbalize their feelings has the effect of reducing the influence of the emotion. Sure, you want people to be passionate about their stance, but that has to be tempered so that they can look around and see the broader picture. Ask, "How do you feel about this?" If they come back with a dispassionate answer, things might be all right. But if you sense a little heightened emotion, whether it is anger or joy, then probe a little deeper until it really starts to show. Ask what they are feeling in this manner: "I sense you're not on board with this. Can you tell me more about that?" The best response is more than just an affirmative; it is one in which they actually name the emotion.

Screw the Facts! Let's Just Argue

When peoples' view on decisions are questioned, they often take a stand. They dig their heels in and won't budge.

You're never going to change an emotional decision with logic. Not while the emotion is still there. You have to give the person an out. This is critical because denying emotions exist makes people internalize them, and that causes them to harden their stance.

When you see an angry person, think frustration or fear and then try to get the person to tell you about it. The approach is soft—I don't call people out directly by saying, "What are you scared of?" That's an attack on them personally, and it makes them look and feel weak. Instead, say something like, "I sense some frustration. Can you tell me about that?" Delivered in a relatively soft tone of voice, those words focus on the issue and not the person.

Once people take a stand, there is no reasoning with them. It is no longer about discussing the issue; it's about winning the argument. This is how *really bad decisions* are made.

Behavior styles influence how people tackle problems and have a lot to do with the amount of emotion involved in decision-making. Domineering people bring a lot of emotion, often anger or relatedness, to the process. Contrast that with the analytic, where a cooler, calmer head is at work. But even analytics can get frustrated, passionate, and caught up in the emotions of the moment. They just rarely show it in an overt way.

When talking to your managers, remember the emotional side. Later, as you develop their trust in you, share what you've been doing to deal with emotions and ask them to follow your example. It's another way to get them engaged in developing their people.

The Process and Experience Are as Important as the Information

Ask any ten experts how to make good decisions, and you'll get twenty-one different answers. We used to teach people to gather all of the facts, sift through them, analyze them using some method like fault-tree analysis, or two columns on a piece of paper (the pros and cons) or any number of other methods. But that isn't how good decision-makers operate. They don't have time to do that.

Decisions are made by comparing options with scenarios from past experiences. Those experiences are rarely just work-related. Often, they come from personal lives, hobbies, and volunteering. When people are inexperienced, they have relatively few things to make comparisons with. The more and broader types of experience a person has, the more information the person has to quickly compare the present situation with. Early on, when managers are new to the position or company, the decision-making process needs to be more formal. As managerial experience is broadened and deepened, they will rely less on a formal process and more on experience. That takes time—and experience. But how to get that experience?

This is where the benefits of cross-training really show up. Often, new managers are assigned to shadow different positions so that "they get a feel for those positions, so they have empathy for the people." But at some point during their stint in other people's shoes, ask them about how they are making decisions now, with this new experience.

How has seeing other people's roles helped them make better decisions?

Good decisions are made by people who envision, *actually mentally play out* the option they think is the best. Cross-training develops broader experiences, giving them more options. They think through the scenario, simulating the process in their minds. They look for what feels right, and where things can go wrong. They look for the unintended consequences. If a scenario doesn't end well, they move on to the next option and play it out as well.

Does this work well all of the time? Of course not. We can never foresee some of the bizarre things that life throws at us.

Which is why it is necessary to elicit others' viewpoints, welcome second opinions, and actually embrace the person who disagrees with you. Well, not actually hug them, but…

Encourage your managers to disagree with you. Make it safe for them to do so. When disagreement reveals a better decision, say so. Then point out that it happened, and your managers might look at using that technique with their own people as a way to make better decisions and build trust.

No Consequences Lead to Poor Decisions

One of the reasons some people continue to make poor decisions is that they don't have to face the consequences. Managers make decisions that labor has to carry out. When a decision turns out to be incorrect, the manager rarely has to face the customer. Yes, he may have to deal with the insurance company and a peer review, but there is nothing like having to face the customer and explain and apologize. There is typically a buffer between management and the person affected by the decision, especially if that person is a client, and that buffer may be the salesperson or even labor.

It's not just about suffering the consequences of a poor decision. It's about learning from them and determining how to handle the decision in the future.

It's probably not just one particular decision at issue. It's probably decision-making in general.

Lead by example. This doesn't mean "Never send anyone to do a job that you wouldn't do yourself" or "Treat people the way that you want to be treated." It means make good decisions and help your people make good decisions. It has been my observation that an organization whose leadership makes poor decisions and ignores potentially poor decisions made by others is doomed to failure. This is because people learn from your example—make poor decisions and deal with the consequences later. I have never understood why some managers and leaders make decisions this way, as it creates a reactive and not a proactive culture.

As they say, crap rolls downhill.

Failure Will Happen—Here's How to Deal with It

It is essential to both the learning process and survival of the company to revisit decisions that failed. Failure will happen. It is how you and your managers deal with failure that will set you apart from the competition—your willingness to look at the information, the process, the work product, and (let me be clear here) *lastly*, the people. Look at everything else first, before you look at the people.

Old pilots have an old saying: "Any landing you walk away from is a good landing." But some of them could be *better* landings. Likewise, you probably remember decisions whose results were, "*Whew.* We got away with that." It's essential to revisit the decisions and ideas that seemed like a good idea at the time. It is possible that better decisions could have been made. Reviewing decisions in the correct manner afterward is *not* second-guessing or Monday morning quarterbacking; it's not micromanaging or assigning fault. Properly reviewing decisions is simply asking, "Could we have done better and if so, how?"

Good decision makers:

- Advance the business toward its goals; they strive for outcomes that are most productive, most efficient, and yield high-quality work
- Take into account the safety of personnel and property
- Recognize and deal with the emotional side of the decision
- Understand that all decisions are made with incomplete and inaccurate information
- Recognize one can never have at hand, nor assimilate and understand, all of the information that may be available to make a decision, and that rarely is all of the information correct, and it can be out of context, making it incorrect for that situation
- Start with a gut-level look at the situation, then actually visualize the outcomes of the different possibilities

›LESSON 7‹
Think Strategically— Act Tactically

Management at every level needs both to understand and foster strategic thinking.

"Take those pliers back to Ace and get the ones from Sears. They're $2 cheaper."

This manager ran a service company that worked in refineries. In refinery maintenance, a common tool, some would argue a required tool, is the adjustable plier. These pliers are to tools as duct tape is to camping gear. They are used as a wrench to tighten nuts, to remove insulation bands on piping, and to open and close special high-pressure valves. These pliers make work faster and easier under difficult circumstances. Every crew has at least two pairs of these pliers.

On Sunday, a crew responded to an emergency call that involved stopping a leak in a valve that was spitting butane inside a refinery. *Nothing like preventing a fire, right?* When the crew arrived to work on the leak, they discovered they only had one pair of pliers. Someone had "borrowed" the other pliers. Soon after starting the repair, the last pair of pliers fell and couldn't be retrieved.

The on-call supervisor sent a runner to a hardware store across the street from the refinery gate. He bought four pair, took two to the crew and brought two to the shop as backup inventory. Done. No problem.

Monday morning, the manager came in and heard what had happened. He knew that controlling the cost of little things was and is crucial to success in business. He then had that runner go to another store where he'd seen the pliers on sale for $2 less. So, the runner bought new pliers, found the crew in the field at a different refinery, swapped out pliers and brought the new/used ones back to the shop. At the shop, he had to clean the pliers and then take all of them back to the hardware store—again, right outside of the refinery gates.

I look back on that scenario and still scratch my head. I pointed out to the manager that the runner, who was being paid $10 an hour, took more than three hours to make the trips, not to mention the cost of paying his payroll taxes, insurance, etc., as well as fuel for the truck, along with the added risk of having an employee in a company vehicle on the road.

That example really makes several points:
- Even experienced, upper-level managers may not know how to think strategically.
- Just as in buying a vehicle, sticker price doesn't reflect true cost.
- Sometimes we have to point out what is obvious to us, but not to others.

- If the word "should" is involved, prepare to be disappointed.
- Strategic thinking is going to require some financial education. They will need to know where they are in the scheme of cash flow.

All bosses I know want their people to think like them. It can happen, but it won't happen overnight.

If you want people to think like you, you're going to have to teach them how you think.

As people move up in rank, their work becomes more strategic, so they need to look at the bigger picture. This is where you come in. You're their mentor, their coach, their Yoda. Start by recognizing that their decision-making is initially going to be based on tactical work—what they used to do to get the job done. Along the way, someone taught them that every job needs to be booked and completed. That is not necessarily so. Teach them to see the bigger picture, to think strategically and act tactically.

Firefighting at Work and in The Wild

We are so distracted by the little things at work—incidents over which we have no control—that we spend very little time actually performing the work that matters most. We miss opportunities that help the organization move forward. Firefighting is one of those distractions.

A great way to get people to understand the concepts of strategic versus tactical is by using the analogy of the firefighter.

Firefighting is a fact of life. Fires crop up everywhere. Forest fires, building fires, fires onboard ships, and of course, all of those fires at work. The fires at work are the incidents that distract us and keep us from dealing with the real issues. The inexperienced and untrained, regardless of their level in an organization, think that every fire must be fought and vanquished. The experienced know that not all fires need to be put out. When you consider the risk to resources and the potential loss of time, energy, productivity, and reputation, it becomes obvious that not all fires can be fought.

As people move up in an organization, they need to learn to see the bigger, wider picture. With your guidance, they can learn which fires are diversions, which are threatening, which fires to monitor, and which to ignore and just let them burn out.

Tactical thinking is about how to fight fires. Strategic thinking is about determining which fires to fight, which to let burn, and taking the time and resources you saved to do something more important: prevent future fires.

The combination—knowing which fires to fight and how to fight them—is crucial.

But why do we even fight fires?

Firefighting is Sexy, But It Doesn't Get the Job Done

Firefighting is a metaphor for the way many people work. Many managers are less than effective because they like to run around putting out fires. Why? Because firefighters are sexy. They can be heroes and tell war stories.

"Yeah! When I walked into that meeting today, everyone was sitting around a conference table the size of an aircraft carrier! Everyone was looking at me like they were sizing me up for dinner. But I remained calm. Smoothly talked them off the ledge and..."

As if going to a meeting with a pissed-off client is the same as crawling through a mile of broken glass to cross the jaws of death, pull the tongue of the devil, quench the fires of hell, then walk away to do it again another day.

Somebody has to meet with the client, but it is best if it doesn't have to get to the point where it's about heroes and villains. Because if you get to that point, *there are always more villains than heroes and in business, no one likes (or likes to be) the villain.* Unless you are an actor, being a good villain doesn't pay the bills.

In reality, only real firefighters are heroes. In every other organization, they're just people in their own little movies.

Prevention is the priority

Delegate these

Monitor these

Ignore these

©Bart Gragg

What Are They Avoiding?

It was a bitterly cold day in the winter of 1986. With two feet of fresh snow on the ground under a clear, bone-chilling sky, the biting wind made it feel like there was nothing between us and the North Pole but a barbed wire fence. As the superintendent, I was in charge of dismantling and removing an entire refinery in Oklahoma. That day, I learned a lesson that will always stick with me. Our mission was to remove the entire refinery and tank farm, sell what equipment we could, and scrap out the rest for recycling. The crew was in the field cutting storage tanks into scrap to be recycled.

I decided to use this as an opportunity to get out of the office and work with the crew. One can stand only so much paperwork. I grabbed a custom-made four-foot-long torch and spent the morning working alongside them. At lunch, we headed back to the warmth of the office building to thaw out. While there, my father called to check on me. He was familiar with my work and what I was up against. When I told him I was working in the field as a burner that day, he asked me one thing: "What are you avoiding doing?"

While the crew liked that I was out there with them in that frigid, vocal-cord freezing cold—it turns out misery really does love company—they liked it even more when they had oxygen and propane for their torches, fuel for the crane, and trucks lined up to take the scrap away. They liked it best when they were set up to be successful. Because it was Sunday, I couldn't do much to affect that, but I could take time to think about the coming week and plan for success.

To this day, whenever I meet a manager or supervisor who acts like a firefighter, I ask, "What are you avoiding doing?" followed by, "Why?"

As the manager and mentor of managers and supervisors, watch them for signs that they are avoiding the real work, whether they're doing so by firefighting or working in their former craft, as opposed to their current craft.

So how do you teach strategic thinking?

If you think about your own experience, you'll come up with many examples, but let's kick-start the thinking with this example.

Fire Prevention is Not Sexy—But It Pays the Bills

Start by asking your managers and supervisors this: Is it costlier to fight a fire, clean up the mess, and then rebuild, or to prevent fires in the first place?

Fire prevention is not sexy. But it's the job. Nowhere in the manager's job description or key accountabilities does it say, "And put out all fires everywhere." Key accountabilities are established to prevent fires. Fires are costly, reflect poorly on the manager and the team as a whole, and are indicators of poor planning, improper prioritization, and bad decision-making.

Firefighting takes focus away from the important tasks, long-term strategies, and key accountabilities. Firefighting causes stress on everyone in the vicinity, not just the people directly involved. External and internal customers worry about whether their needs will be met by the department involved with the fire.

Loss of focus, stress and customer worries lead to poor morale and unsuccessful departments and organizations. It is the manager's job to set people up for success by planning for it.

›LESSON 8‹

Piss-Poor Planning on Your Part Does Not Make It an Emergency on My Part

Proper planning creates efficiency, quality, profitability, safety, and so forth, to be sure. The unintended consequences of *not* planning can reach areas that you might not imagine. The *intentional* consequences of proper planning include the number one thing employees ask for at work—clarity. Planning also fosters agreement between managers and their managers, allows managers and employees alike to have a voice, and sets the stage for conversations, which in turn causes a boost in self-esteem and morale, which then leads to an increase in safety and reduced risk.

How to Plan Properly

Bear this in mind: *Planning is simply having conversations and making a series of decisions based on those conversations*

1. **Determine the scope of work.** This step will dictate the extent of planning required. If you're

talking about simply replacing a pump motor, a general discussion and outline of work can be done rather quickly. If you're talking about anchor chain retrieval, total planning time could have taken as much as two hours, but that time could have been spread over several days because the planners would have talked to crane and tug operators, safety coordinators, and (of course) the entire crew.

2. **Start early.** Even simple planning needs start early. The earlier you start, the more time everyone has to think it through, with each person envisioning what the task will take each step of the way, catching potential inefficiencies and safety issues before they happen. If you are talking about a refinery shutdown and turnaround, that planning starts as much as *years* ahead of time and involves planning and revisions right up until the last minute. As you can imagine, communication and decision-making required for that scope of work are tremendous.

3. **Ask questions until you annoy the crap out of people.** Ask "How?" a lot. *How are we going to do this? How are we going to do that? How are they going to...?* Be relentless. *"How will we do this safely? Efficiently?"*

4. **Ask "Who is responsible for that operation?"** Then go find those people and annoy them until they can tell you with confidence when they will be available, what they see as the timeframe for completion of their work, what resources they will bring, and what resources they need you to furnish.

5. **Write it down.** Don't allow anybody to keep critical information in their heads. That's a recipe for, "I forgot."

I advocate the use of the One Page Business Plan (OPBP) when teaching business unit managers. The OPBP offers the following benefits:

- **Simplicity.** It's not complicated.
- **Flexibility.** Plans change for many reasons. The market changes, the economy changes, clients change, etc. This flexible plan makes it easy to adapt.
- **Scalability.** You can get your message to many different levels in your organization. In turn, your managers can easily make sure they are in alignment with company goals.
- **Accountability.** A properly executed plan with objectively measurable key accountabilities makes it easy to manage by fact.
- **Agreement.** Done properly, both you and the managers you manage have a say in what needs to be done and how it will get done.

- **No surprises.** You already hold monthly planning meetings, right? Well, you can use this method to review progress and eliminate the annual employee review. Unless you just love doing those anyway . . .

If They Can't Gantt, Teach Them

For project planning, use Gantt charts. If you don't know how to create and use a Gantt chart, learn. They look complicated. They aren't (unless you pay attention to the idiots on the internet who make them seem complicated—they just want you to either pay them money to teach you or be as miserable as they are because they don't understand them).

Gantt charts are easy. They are bar charts. Screw using Excel or other spreadsheets until you understand the full workings of the chart. Use a good, old-fashioned lead pencil and a large piece of graph paper taped to the wall or conference table. One of the great advantages to this approach is that people get to use more than one learning modality to create the chart. (Learn more in Lesson 10, "Observations From The Field.")

A simple but proper Gantt chart gives everyone input and visibility about the time and resources required for various operations required to complete a project. It also lays out the timelines for ongoing operations.

The Perils of Planning

There are pitfalls with any kind of planning at work, including using Gantt charts, or so they say. Actually, the pitfalls lie within the humans using them, but that holds true for all planning. The pitfalls include:

- A tendency to fudge the numbers in an attempt to underpromise and overdeliver

- People feeling as if the planning process is meant to set them up as the fall person in the event things don't go the way they were planned

- Getting fixated on achieving the goal; sometimes it's better to change the goal than the method of achieving the goal

But if you train your managers to have conversations, these pitfalls, by and large, go away. In one meeting which included four department heads, two working supervisors, and two top leaders. They were planning to remove a major piece of equipment from a ship while it was anchored.

At first, any attempt to get them to talk about what the job required was met with, "Joe knows," or, "We don't need to talk about it. We all help each other out. If I need something, I just go get them [other supervisors] and tell them." As I looked at "them," it was clear they were saying "Yes, but no."

I asked how that affected their jobs. "Well, of course, we'll support him, but we seem to always have to drop what we're doing, what we had planned for that day or week, and go handle his stuff. Sometimes we get the call for help, and he's not ready for us. Then we have to regroup to refocus on our stuff."

Over several planning sessions, the picture became clearer. Faces lit up. People began to see the whole picture. They had started out thinking tactically, not strategically. They needed both. They were finally able to see how their efforts affected each other. They came to their own realizations about what was important and what wasn't.

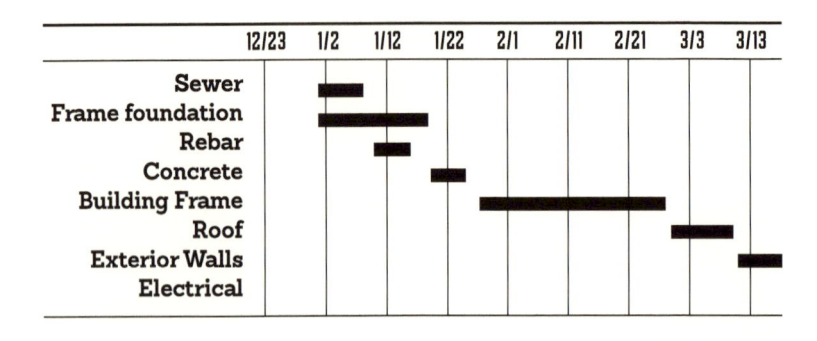

	12/23	1/2	1/12	1/22	2/1	2/11	2/21	3/3	3/13
Sewer		▬							
Frame foundation		▬▬▬							
Rebar			▬						
Concrete				▬					
Building Frame					▬▬▬▬▬				
Roof								▬	
Exterior Walls									▬
Electrical								▬▬▬	

This is a basic Gantt Chart. You can write in data such as manpower, equipment, etc. Remember the advantages of doing this by hand—conversations and agreement.

Why People Dislike Planning

If planning is so good and so helpful, why do so few people do it?

Other than the myth that plans and planning sessions are required to be long and complicated, these are some of the top reasons people resist planning:

- They don't know how to plan.
- It involves decision-making.
- Somebody might hold them accountable.
- People don't have access to all of the data they need.
- Planning is costly.
- Plans change.

Why put in all that effort up front just to have to change things along the way?

The reasons for resistance are either lack of knowledge about the process, or not putting in the effort to visualize and articulate results.

The truth is that proper planning is not complicated. It does take effort, though. As a front-line manager, planning is relatively simple. The higher up one moves in an organization, the more complex the moving parts. Therefore, plans become more complicated (or so people think).

But if you break a business unit down into its individual components, then create a plan for each component, the last bit of real work that has to happen is to make sure that the plans for each business unit not only provide for that unit but that they also support the master plan for the business.

Remember the old saying, "Piss poor planning on your part doesn't make it an emergency on my part." That actually works up and down the food chain.

Planning:
- creates efficiency
- promotes comradery
- promotes bigger picture thinking
- makes it easy to manage by fact
- promotes safety and morale

›LESSON 9‹
Does Safety Really Begin With Leadership?

I was having a conversation with a young man named Del, a man who had the potential to have as much impact on a customer as any other person in the company. Del was a parts counterman. He wasn't on the fast track to promotion, but he was determined to do his job and do it the right way. Del was going to take care of his customers.

Things hadn't been going so well at his company. Parts weren't being ordered or delivered in a timely manner. Management didn't want to tell the customer for fear of any number of things, egg on their face being one of them. Del knew they had to be told, though, so he quietly contacted his customers and let them know their options. Finally, Del decided it was time to talk to management. The worst they could do was get pissed and fire him. But he'd had enough.

I asked Del what the results were.

Paraphrasing Del, "My customers were rolling their eyes and walking out when I told them their parts weren't going to arrive on time. Plus, maintenance had fallen, and the place wasn't looking too good. Morale was headed down, as you know.

"But things have gotten a lot better here since people started telling the truth.

"Management *needs* to hear the truth, don't you think? When management started hearing the truth, things started getting better. My customers are smiling now."

And this little extra gem:

"My company may not be the best, but that should not keep me from being my best."

Culture—Not Just Important to Yogurt

Why was Del able to approach his boss? Because our work together had taught them one of the hidden meanings behind the phrase, "Safety Begins with Leadership."

You see that slogan everywhere in the blue-collar segments of industry. Ask anyone what it means, and you get the same three answers:

- Leadership must provide a safe place to work.
- Leadership must give us the safety equipment and training we need.
- Leadership must walk the talk and lead by example.

All good answers, but there is a deeper meaning that in itself can lead to greater safety and production and fewer incidents. So, what does "Safety begins with leadership" really mean? The best way to answer that is with this sentence: "Management makes this place safe enough to tell the truth."

Safety Begins with Leadership: "Management makes this place safe enough to tell the truth."

You want your people to feel safe enough to tell you the truth, and preferably to do so before an incident could happen, or (at the worst) as soon as it happens.

You want your managers to make good decisions. They need accurate and timely information. To get that, their people need to tell the truth. And the culture of the organization will dictate whether that will happen. Leadership needs to create a safe place to tell the truth.

A reminder: Their team is a reflection of their leadership, Your team is a reflection of your leadership.

Change from "Who" to "How?"

Make it safe for people to say what they need to say. People need to know they won't be dismissed, rejected, ridiculed, ostracized, embarrassed, or otherwise made to feel stupid.

And how do you do that? It's simple, really. Keep these two words top of mind: Be *respectful* and use the word *how*.

How?

First, here is why we use the word "how." If you have ever experienced the question, "Who did that," then you already know the results. That question alone causes a drop in morale that gets buried deeper than Wile E. Coyote's ACME anvil falling off a cliff. It is the phrase that announces, "Let the witch hunt begin!" At that point, everyone runs for cover. If they can't get away from the inquisition, they start covering their asses. People clam up. If they speak, it is to deny anything or lay blame elsewhere.

You never get to the truth.

So never, ever, *ever* start with "Who did this," even if *this* is a good thing.

Also, never start with, "Why?" The reason is rooted in everyone's childhood. Mom or Dad comes home and finds cookie crumbs on the floor, or broken glass on the counter—whatever. It's happened to all of us. Maybe you're alone, or your big sister is pointing at you. But it's obvious who did it. So, they ask you "*Why* did you…?"

You just know that regardless of the answer, you're in trouble.

I'm not saying *never* ask why. I'm saying be careful how and when you ask it. Never make it an accusation. When you get to the point at which asking why is a necessity, you have to get to a place of calmness you may never have felt. Your voice is normal, conversational. Your body language projects peace; all is right with the world. You say, "I'm just curious here. Why did you do that? I want to know more about how you think. It's OK. We're not talking about you getting in trouble. I am simply curious about how you make decisions."

Notice that last line. You are *curious about how they make decisions*. That's one way to use the word *how* to make a person feel safe enough to tell you the truth.

> LESSON 10 <
Observations From the Field

They're Managers—Now What?

Management isn't static. Leadership isn't static. All of the successes I have had in my career are due to movement. Early on a lot of that movement was due to pain because I didn't know how to manage.

Some of the pain was the result of bad decisions.

Most of my epic fails, the ones that haunt me, are due to inaction. Inaction is the fear of failure or inability to make a decision.

Not being static isn't just about not moving—it's about moving in the right direction more often than not. A *lot* more often than not.

Success in management and leadership happens when managers actively develop themselves and their people, and they grow and move together in the right direction.

Management Styles

While much has been written about management styles, it never hurts to take a fresh look at them.

- **Management by title.** The "Do it because I said so!" or "My way or the highway!" style of management causes resentment. Morale falls quickly with these types of managers. This is the default of most new managers. The key to success is to get them past this phase as quickly as possible
- **Hands-off.** These managers are indecisive, uncommunicative, and all but invisible.
- **Part-time manager.** They're in, they're out. Who knows when they'll show up, even when they're at work.
- **Only-when-I-need-something-from-you manager.** The name says it all. They are in it for themselves and have no credibility because they don't care about their people.
- **Micromanager.** The root of this management style is insecurity.
- **Whatever it takes.** Be careful that these managers don't add, "no matter the cost."
- **R.I.P. manager (retired in place).** This manager gave up for any one of a dozen reasons, including incompetence and company culture.

On Training Blue Collar Managers and Supervisors

Your Role in Developing Your People: First Coach, Then Mentor

The most effective way to teach is to coach and then switch to mentoring. Coaching as I use the term here is like coaching sports—give direction and show how it's done. Mentoring is like being Yoda—making appropriate statements and asking questions to make people think. The point at which you switch from coaching to mentoring is when students begin to put the pieces together, think through the process, and see it on their own. Switching to mentoring will require trust, because it means you'll be asking more questions, and student needs to know that you are asking not to find fault, but to help them think.

One method that can be used to help establish and maintain trust is to say, "Many people get scared or lock up when they are asked questions. This is because, in their past, they saw questions as a means to find fault or embarrass them. That is not at all why I would like to ask you questions. In this case, though, I want to ask questions so that I can better understand you and where you are. And sometimes I will ask questions that might make you uncomfortable. I don't mean to do that, but discomfort is based on fear of feeling like you should know the answer when you may not. It's OK not to know everything. So, hearing what I just said, are you okay with me asking you some questions?"

How People Learn

When I ask about the actual transition from labor into management, from field into the office, I hear the broom closet story. "It feels like I was given a computer on a desk in a broom closet. They handed me a four-inch thick, three-ring binder which supposedly had everything I would ever need, and maybe a phone list of people I have never heard of. I was supposed to call them if I had any questions. Boy, did I ever have questions! But I never called because I felt it would make me look stupid. They'd just tell me to read the damn book anyway. Then I started getting emails demanding this report or that report or asking me why this wasn't done, or when that is going to get done. That was my first week of training."

Remember when moving from labor into management, people change from working primarily with tools and objects to working primarily with people and data. This requires broadening neural pathways to the previously lesser-used areas of the brain. Just as important, though, is to recognize that you are also asking people to learn in a different way. When people train for and perform tasks as laborers and technicians, they learn by watching others, asking questions for clarification, listening to stories others tell, paying attention to the sounds and the feel of the tools and objects they work with.

Blue-collar people learn in a way which may be different than the way you want them to learn now. They are now being asked to sit still and read a manual, and to both process and communicate information differently.

If you were to research how people learn, you might hear the term "learning modalities" or "learning styles." You might see words like kinesthetic, tactile, auditory, and so forth. The problem with those terms is that the definitions are frequently confusing and the properties of each may cross boundaries (not to mention you have to learn a whole new language).

To simplify matters and make the terms more user-friendly, I consulted with Beth Mermann, a retired learning specialist. From discussions with her, I came up with a list of hints and terms to describe the various ways people learn. Bear in mind that most people learn in a combination of two or more ways.

- **Walkers** pace or walk while thinking and/or talking. The movement helps them process what they are learning or thinking about.

- **Talkers** have to talk it out—that is, they process by going over everything verbally, often stopping and asking questions, some of which may be rhetorical. Then they answer it themselves and move on to the next potential sequence of events. Sometimes they walk and talk.

- **Readers and Writers** write words, ideas, and concepts down, which helps to cement things in their minds. This is actually one of the more universal ways of getting people to learn and to process information. It's why we use notebooks with everyone. They may also like blueprints, flowcharts, instruction manuals, and so forth.

- **Doodlers and Drawers** like creating images, shapes, and drawings. When they try to explain something, you might see them drawing it out on paper, on a whiteboard, with a pencil on a piece of wood, a stick in the dirt, and so forth.

- **Visual learners** like seeing things in action. They want you to show them, or to see useful videos that show the process.
- **Thinkers** like to mentally visualize the process before attempting it.
- **Listeners** learn by hearing themselves talk it out, or by hearing others tell them about it.
- **Doers** learn by attempting the task at hand, especially if it involves something physical.
- **Sensors** learn by feeling their way through a situation with intuition as opposed to trying to know the answer before moving forward.

There are a great many ways to make training more effective. While trying to get a group of managers to understand how to track revisions when editing Word documents, I created a screen capture video which included a narration of the process. We posted this video and posted it on the company's YouTube channel. In another instance, we created a whiteboard video training for hazard communication and made it specific to the client's needs. Both of these methods combine several of the learning types referred to above.

A word of caution: While the two examples above used technology to help explain how to perform a task, use tech sparingly, or you'll find people grow resistant to it. You don't want to create an electronic babysitter for your learners.

If you have the opportunity to bring your team together to plan an event such as moving a ship, replacing a piece of equipment, rearranging a warehouse, or really any simple to complex process, creating a Gantt chart using graph paper, not an electronic tool, helps individuals and teams visualize, discuss, and document the priorities and interactions. Some of the hidden power is that the process of creating the chart lends itself to helping almost all of the different learning styles to fully understand what is happening.

Volumes have been written on training methods. Be careful that you don't find one method that works one time and think that's the key to all future training. To be effective, you will need to mix it up and train differently to see which method sticks with the individual. The key will be to observe how your people learn, and train them using matching methods.

›LESSON 11‹
Selecting for Success

Ann was a grandmother, a leader in inside sales for many years for an independent insurance company. Per company policy, she had topped out in her salary and compensation range.

Ann couldn't make any more money where she was. Her boss, Todd, was concerned for her. In January, Todd asked Ann whether she might want to go into outside sales, as he could no longer increase her salary in her current position. She agreed. In March, it was very clear that the situation was not only not working as expected—it was failing miserably. Ann would come into the office in the morning, and it was clear that she didn't want to leave. She did make appointments but never closed any deals.

I asked Todd how Ann had sold when she was in inside sales. He told me that she was great at recognizing opportunities when people called into the office. Prospects would call, and she was able to help them figure out what best fit their needs. Working with existing clients, she was outstanding. She recognized an opportunity to upsell them and would do so easily. I asked for more about that. "Well," he said, "she would be on the phone with them and ask after their family and hear that someone had a baby or grandbaby. Then she'd ask whether they had considered upping their life insurance policy since they now had an extra family member. That kind of thing."

Todd sighed and said, "What do I do with this? How could this have happened?"

The problem was a conflict between the position and the person.

Here's the breakdown of what happened with Ann from a behavioral and motivational standpoint. This is how the job and the person either fit or are misfits.

Ann was naturally inclined to go to the same place every day. She enjoyed the consistency of her surroundings. She didn't actually *sell* anyone anything, despite what you may think. She *took care of people*. She was looking out for them. When Ann was assigned to outside sales, she then had to go against her natural behavior style and internal motivation. Now she was being asked to change her physical location every day. She now thought she had to sell—something that was the opposite, to her, of *taking care of people*. She had to meet new people in their domain, not hers. She didn't have time or the ability to warm up a relationship and get to know people. In outside sales, Ann was entirely outside of her comfort zone. In inside sales, she had always done what was natural for her—taking care of people, not selling.

Todd finally asked me, "Why did she take the position if money wasn't an issue for her?" Believe it or not, the answer is as simple as this: When your boss comes to you and says, "I can't pay you more where you are. Your option is to go to a different position," what people hear is, "This is the opportunity I have for you. If you don't take it, I'll be disappointed in you, and that might affect your future here."

Most people are hired or promoted based on two criteria—likeability and past performance. They are great at their current *technical* craft or trade; they get along well with their coworkers, and we like them. In the financial world, they have fine print that also holds true in selecting people: *past performance is no guarantee of future returns.* Nowhere is this truer than in the transition from blue-collar labor to management.

Let's look at this business of selecting managers differently. If managers even take time to think about hiring or promoting, they think about skill sets they want their employees to have—usually the hard skills (like knowing Microsoft Office, being able to lift fifty pounds, run faster than a speeding bullet, and leap over tall buildings in a single bound). Those are important skills that need to be listed. But in combination with those hard skills are the behaviors and motivational characteristics required to be successful in a position. We're going to start by asking what *people traits* a position requires.

The Core of the Selection Process

Think of the selection process as a jigsaw puzzle. The best way to put one together is to find all of the corner pieces, then the edge pieces, and then to assemble them. After that, the internal parts, the real subject, becomes clearer.

In the selection case, the corners are:
1. Key accountabilities
2. Hard or technical skills
3. Behavior
4. Internal Motivation

If those are the four corners of the puzzle, then the edges are simply the details that go along with each of the corners. Finally, you have the center, which is now a much clearer picture of the qualities and attributes of the person the job requires to be most successful.

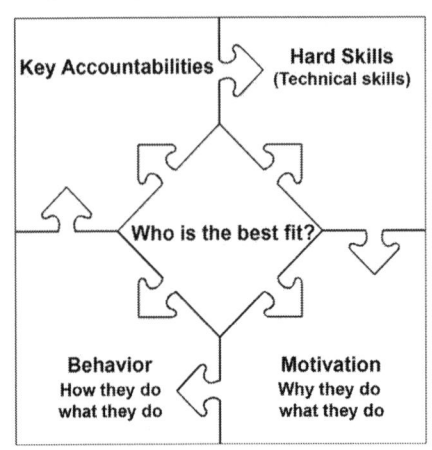

```
Key Accountabilities        Hard Skills
                            (Technical skills)

            Who is the best fit?

Behavior                    Motivation
How they do                 Why they do
what they do                what they do
```

The corner pieces represent what the job itself requires for the best outcomes.

The center represents the person that best fits those characteristics.

© Bart Gragg

The key is to look at the *position*, not the *person*. Looking at the position offers two advantages: it helps marry behavior and motivation with the primary tasks required for success, and it helps remove bias toward (or against) a given individual. In order for this approach to work, you'll need to dig out those key accountabilities you developed earlier. Or start from scratch.

Once you have the key accountabilities in hand, *do* think about people. But don't think about any *one* individual. You still want the candidate to be an unknown entity. The way you want to think about people at this point is to think about behavior (how the job needs to be done) and motivation (what an individual would value in the job). What is it about the job that would make them want to do it and do it well?

Now you're off to find the person who meets those criteria. Most often, it will be easier to see whether a candidate understands and agrees with the key accountabilities and has the required hard skills. What might be a little more difficult is matching the candidate's behavior and motivation. If they snap right into place, all good. That would be rare, though. No one will be a perfect fit, but some will come closer than others.

If you have to force things, trimming here, leaving gaps there, then it's time to think about how hard it would be to fit that person into the role, taking the long view (you are going to be in business for a while, right?). What kind of effort are you willing to make to fit them? Alternatively, you could look elsewhere to see whether there may be another person available who fits a little more readily.

What If They Can't Hack It?

What if someone you promote to supervision or management doesn't make it?

Usually, this happens for several reasons, such as:
- They are unable to grasp and implement management concepts.
- They grasp the concepts but realize management isn't for them at this time.
- They don't want to put effort and discipline into learning the craft of the new position.

In most cases, people in such situations are either fired as incompetent, or they quit out of frustration. Rarely do they return to their old positions. That is seen as a demotion. Instead, it needs to be seen as an opportunity to *keep good talent*. In fact, viewed in the right light, it's an opportunity to keep even better talent.

In either case, you lose a good if not great employee.

So why risk losing them?

Why not make it easy to keep them?

After I had worked six months with one group of potential and current supervisors in a service company in Texas, one participant, Jeff, decided he didn't want the job as a supervisor. I knew he had the potential, but *at that time* he didn't want to make the switch. His employer let him go back to the field. Several months later I asked the owner how Jeff was doing. He said "He's one of my best employees. Because of your training, he now sees things in a different light. He can see the bigger picture and is an advocate for us with other field people. He recognizes when something may become an issue and brings it to our attention."

If you've ever asked yourself, "Why can't they think like an owner?"

They can.

So don't can them.

›RESOURCES‹

As you might imagine, this book could go on forever, and neither of us would ever get our work done. So, instead of writing more here, the following resources are all available at www.bluecollaru.com/resources and may interest you. There you will find links to more information on some of the subject matter in this book as well as other, different information, free downloadable forms for your internal use, suggested reading, and the services Blue Collar University offers.

Articles and Blog Posts on Topics Such as:

Getting Rid of the Dreaded Annual Review

Where's the Money? Getting managers and supervisors acquainted with true cost versus sticker price.

Consultation Services

Working within an organization to better understand, develop, and support managers and supervisors.

Setting up internal training systems.

Keynotes, Workshops and Programs:

"They're Managers – Now What? How to Develop Blue Collar Managers and Supervisors"
Amazing how this has the same title as this book, right?

"Cracking the Manager Code – 11 Traits of Effective Managers and Supervisors"
And, ahem, leaders, of course.

"True North – A Look at the Past For a View of the Future"
Never start with a blank sheet of paper—start with this method for looking at lessons learned and using them to move forward.

Blue Collar Bootcamp.
A simple, powerful training process to get managers and supervisors off to a running start.

Communication for Managers and Supervisors.
This workshop is an in-depth look at how the individual affects communication.

Decision Making and Planning for Managers and Supervisors.

Custom training for management and leadership.

Recommended Reading List

An ongoing list of reading material for leaders and managers use to develop themselves.

Free Downloads, Worksheets and Cheat-sheets like "Can't We Just Get Along?" which helps others understand your management and communication styles and preferences.

〉ABOUT THE AUTHOR 〈

Bart Gragg knows from personal experience the pain managers and *their* managers go through when they have not been taught what their job entails or given the tools to accomplish it. He understands that their managers are also frustrated. He created Blue Collar University to help all managers better understand how to work with each other more productively.

Bart has worked in some of the toughest industries out there—from living on drilling rigs during oil and gas exploration, to heavy industrial dismantling, refinery repair, and pipeline construction. He has a B.S. in Geology, is a Certified Professional Behaviors Analyst, holds the CHST (Construction Health and Safety Technician) and OHST (Occupational Hygiene and Safety Technician) certificates, and is a Certified Executive One Page Business Plan consultant.

Made in the USA
Columbia, SC
22 December 2019